MODERN TIMES

The Cold War

S R Gibbons

Longman

LONGMAN GROUP UK LIMITED
Longman House, Burnt Mill, Harlow, Essex CM20 2JE, England
and Associated Companies throughout the world.

Published in the United States of America
by Longman Inc., New York

© Longman Group UK Limited 1986

First published 1986
Second impression 1987

ISBN 0 582 22366 0

Set in 11/12pt Linotron Baskerville

*Produced by Longman Group (FE) Limited
Printed in Hong Kong*

British Library Cataloguing in Publication Data
Gibbons, S.R.
    The Cold War. — (Modern times)
    1. World politics — 1945–   2. Communist
    countries — Foreign relations
    I. Title   II. Series
    327'.09171'3   D840

    ISBN 0–582–22366–0

Library of Congress Cataloging in Publication Data
Gibbons, S.R.
    The Cold War.
    (Modern times)
    Includes index.
    Summary: Discusses the features of the period after
World War II during which the Communist nations and the
democratic nations were engaged in a tense relationship
which never evolved into fighting and was marked by the
spread of communism, increased spying, and, ultimately,
detente.
    1. World politics — 1945–   — Juvenile literature.
[1. World politics — 1945–   ]   I. Title.   II. Series:
Modern times (Harlow, Essex)
D843.G448   1986   909.82   85–23907

ISBN 0–582–22366–0

Contents

Contents

Preface

The story of the Cold War is enormously complex — so much so that any 'simple' view of it can only be misleading. This book covers the major features, as most Western historians would see them, of the years 1945 to 1968. A few significant themes such as arms control or détente have been carried beyond the latter date in order to stress their continued relevance for our modern world.

Where feasible, the main actors in the Cold War drama have been allowed to speak for themselves. Similarly, I have tried to enliven the text with detailed narrative or descriptive passages, based on primary sources. However, readers should know that such material is much more plentiful for events in the West than for those in the USSR. For example, many independent accounts throw light on the vital decision-making processes of the Western nations at times of special tension. Comparable material from the USSR is not available.

In marrying the obvious Cold War themes with a roughly chronological chapter arrangement it has been impossible to avoid occasional repetition or discontinuity. Careful use of the contents list will enable readers to select the episodes which interest them, and to order them as they wish.

The subject is of the most crucial importance for our times. The book should be of use to anyone wanting a reasonably straightforward account of its essentials.

S. R. Gibbons

The new map of eastern Europe after 1945. The USSR had gained territory from Romania, Czechoslovakia, Poland and Germany; it had also swallowed up Lithuania, Latvia and Estonia. The heavy line is the 'Iron Curtain', dividing East from West

1 Wartime Allies Fall Out

The Last Months of the Second World War: April–August 1945

In April 1945 Germany and Japan faced defeat, with their navies and air forces shattered and their armies on the retreat. The Allied nations which had struggled to master them had built up overwhelming strength. They insisted that the Germans and the Japanese should surrender unconditionally. This meant that no 'deals' could be made — the victors would have complete power to decide the fate of Germany and Japan.

Germany's great cities had been ruined by tremendous bombing attacks. The remnants of the German armies — still over 6,000,000 strong — were fighting desperately to repel invaders from German soil. From the east and south-east came the Soviet Red Army. From the west came American, British, Canadian and French armies. The Western Allies overran all western and central Germany, and thrust even into Czechoslovakia and Austria.

Link-up on the Elbe: Albert Kotzebue meets a Soviet General

It seemed likely that a link-up between Soviet soldiers from the east and Americans from the west would occur somewhere well to the south of Berlin. To avoid possible clashes, the armies in this area were told to halt — the Soviet 1st Ukrainian Group at the river Elbe, and the Americans at one of the Elbe's tributaries, the river Mulde. Forty-five kilometres separated the American and Soviet forces. On the American side, young officers were anxious to be first to meet the Russians.

1

23 April. Sergeant Alex Balter was operating his portable radio on channel 4160: 'American forces approaching south Germany. Listen, Russian forces! This is the voice of your American allies now at Mittweida, awaiting a meeting with you.' He repeated his message over and over. Then a Soviet voice broke in: 'Bravo Americansky! Bravo Americansky!' only to be blotted out quickly by a German song. Later in the day Balter again made radio contact. The two armies, from opposite sides of the world, were almost in touch!

25 April. Lieutenant Albert Kotzebue, of the US 69th Division, set out from the Mulde river with seven jeeps. His orders were to patrol eastwards for up to 3 kilometres. The countryside was quiet. Villagers stayed behind locked doors. The patrol met a group of about seventy German soldiers who were glad to surrender. They were disarmed and sent marching back to the American main positions. At one farmhouse, when Albert cautiously pushed the door open with his rifle he found the farmer, his wife and three children all seated at a table, dead. They had taken poison.

The patrol pushed further and further eastwards, breaking orders. But Albert's determination paid off. In the village of Leckwitz, the patrol came upon a horseman in a fur hat. He was a Red Army cavalryman, and told the Americans his unit was still on the Elbe. The jeeps pushed on, to reach the river near Strelha. The Elbe is about 300 metres wide here, but on the eastern bank Albert could see soldiers in unfamiliar uniforms. Attempts to call them by radio failed. Albert had two green flares fired: the Americans' recognition signal. There was no response.

The American patrol searched the river bank and found a small boat. Albert set out with four men, using rifle butts as oars. On the eastern bank he was greeted by Soviet infantry, and was soon being photographed with Soviet officers. Albert's day finished with a Soviet-American banquet in a farmhouse. He was sitting bare-footed by the fire, drying his wet socks, when a Soviet general arrived to meet him.

Similar meetings occurred during the next few days, and after the German surrender. The Second World War had brought America and the USSR face to face, in the heart of Germany.

American and Russian soldiers at Torgau, on the River Elbe, 25 April 1945. Private Joe Polawsky, the American standing in the jeep, tried hard throughout the Cold War years to revive the good feeling of the wartime meeting. He went to see Khrushchev, and sought out some of the Soviet soldiers he had first met in 1945, urging that the two nations should be friends

1945: East meets West in Central Europe: Diary of the Vital Events

7 March	American forces cross the Rhine, Germany's natural barrier in the west.
13 April	Soviet forces complete the capture of Vienna, the Austrian capital.
16 April	Soviet armies in great strength cross the river Oder, Germany's natural barrier in the east.
30 April	Hitler commits suicide in his underground bunker as Soviet forces storm central Berlin.
4 May	German forces in north-west Germany surrender to the British.
7 May	Most of Austria in Soviet and American hands: Germans in western Austria surrender to the Americans.
8 May	Resistance in Germany ceases.
11 May	German forces in Czechoslovakia surrender to Soviet and American armies.

The Alliance Holds

As the war had worsened for Germany it had been Hitler's dream that his enemies would fall out. He predicted repeatedly that the Western Allies — mainly Britain and the USA — would quarrel with their Soviet partners, and the 'unnatural' alliance against Germany be broken. But this did not happen. The 'Big Three' held firmly to their alliance, and to their determination not to make peace separately.

With the end of the war in Europe, American, Soviet, British and French forces occupied the whole of Germany, and began the immense task of restoring some sort of order and organisation.

The Occupation Zones in Germany

It had been planned in 1944 to divide Germany between the Western and Soviet forces. As it happened, the areas conquered by the armies corresponded roughly with those allotted to them. The Red Army moved forward in Germany to occupy a stretch of country which the British and Americans had taken; and the Americans pulled their troops out of Czechoslovakia. Both armies moved forward from their final positions of 8 May to complete the occupation of Austria.

The arrangements for the occupation zones went without a hitch. But their victory meant that the Allies had many other pressing problems to face. The most serious ones were discussed at two important conferences. The first was at Yalta, three months before the final victory; the second was at Potsdam, just after the German surrender.

Allied Conferences at Yalta and Potsdam

The Big Three meet at Yalta

During the night of 2 February 1945 the airfield at Luqa in Malta was exceptionally busy. At ten minute intervals large transport planes roared down the runway and took off into the Mediterranean night. By early dawn twenty American Skymasters and five Yorks of the RAF were in the air, carrying about 700 British and US politicians, service chiefs,

4

The post-war occupation zones of Germany and Austria. The dashed border is the Oder-Neisse line, cutting off the German provinces of Pomerania and Silesia. Berlin and Vienna were each under four-power control

advisers and officials. Among them were the American President, Roosevelt, and the British Prime Minister, Churchill.

The armada of planes flew due east for three and a half hours, then turned north. They crossed first the Aegean Sea, then parts of Turkey, and finally the Black Sea. After seven hours they had covered about 2240 kilometres. Eventually

5

they landed on a runway freshly cleared of snow at Saki airport, in the Crimea. They had arrived in the USSR. Churchill watched as the crippled US President was helped down from the special lift which had been fitted to his personal Skymaster, *Sacred Cow*. There was a welcome from the waiting Russians, and lavish refreshments. Then a long convoy of cars set off for the seaside town of Yalta. All the way, on the five-hour drive, Red Army soldiers stood at the roadside. Many of them were girls, armed with tommy guns. Here and there the travellers saw burned-out buildings, or derelict tanks. Until nine months before, the Crimea had been held by the Germans.

The cars passed through the mountains of the southern Crimea. Then they left the snow behind, and dropped down to the shores of the Black Sea. Here, said one of the British party, 'we were in a different country. Much warmer, cypress trees and villages with nice tiled roofs — rather like Italy.'

The Yalta area, with its mild climate and striking sea views, has many beautiful villas and palaces. They were built for the wealthy in pre-Revolution days. Stalin was based in one of these, and Churchill was housed in another. Roosevelt and his senior staff were given the Livadia Palace, which had formerly belonged to the Tsar Nicholas 11. In February 1945 the three powers held their meetings in the Livadia palace so that Roosevelt would not have to travel.

The Russians had made enormous efforts in preparation. Armies of workmen had repaired the buildings. Decorations and furniture had been brought from Moscow. Waiters had been transferred from the two or three best Moscow hotels. The food provided was sumptuous — a sort of perpetual banquet. Once, remembered Churchill, 'somebody said casually that there was no lemon peel in the cocktails. The next day a lemon tree loaded with fruit was growing in the hall.'

The Western Allies had also made preparations. In the harbour at Sebastopol were anchored American and British ships which served as communication links. Mosquito aircraft daily made the dangerous flight across Europe to bring vital mail from London. The President and the Prime Minister were in constant touch with Washington and London. The scene was set for a major 'Big Three' conference to shape the post-war world.

Difficulties over Poland

The conference lasted eight days. There were some difficult discussions, but agreement was reached on most subjects. By far the greatest problem was Poland. How free was Poland to be, after the war? Churchill and Roosevelt wanted to be sure that Poland would be 'free and independent'. The country had already been partly liberated. There was a Polish government in exile in London, waiting to take over. But the advancing Russians had set up another Polish government at Lublin, in the area freed of Germans. This Lublin government was a communist one. Stalin made clear the USSR's strong feeling over Poland:

'For the Russian people, the question of Poland is not only a question of honour but also a question of security. Throughout history, Poland has been the corridor through which the enemy has passed into Russia. Twice in the last thirty years our enemies, the Germans, have passed through this corridor.'

The USSR, he said, must have a friendly government in Poland. However, James Byrnes, one of the American party, commented that 'their idea of a friendly government is a government completely dominated by them'.

Churchill was particularly worried over Poland, for Britain had gone to war in 1939 over Germany's invasion of the country. Both he and Roosevelt wanted democratic elections, like those held in western countries, to take place.

The Yalta Decisions

The conference made a number of decisions.

1 The Allies would go on together to defeat Germany, and then disarm her.
2 Plans for a United Nations Organisation would be completed at a special conference in San Francisco in April 1945. In this new world organisation, the Allies would each be able to veto any proposed UN action.

7

3 The USSR would join the war against Japan within three months of Germany's defeat.
4 Germany would be split into four zones between the three powers and France. The French zone, the USSR insisted, would be cut out of those at first allocated to Britain and America.
5 Germany would be made to pay reparations to the Allies, in the form of machinery and other basic equipment to compensate them for the losses of the war. Stalin wanted to fix the total amount at twenty million dollars' worth, but the Western Allies thought this impossibly large. The amount was left to be decided later.
6 Poland: the communist government which had been set up by the Soviets at Lublin in the wake of the Red Army would be 'reorganised in a more democratic way'. It would include non-communists. 'Free and unfettered elections' should then be held, with all parties except pro-Nazi ones able to take part.
7 Poland's new border should be fixed at the Curzon line in the east.

No agreement was possible on Poland's western border; this was left for settlement at a later peace conference.

Potsdam, July 1945

The Allies met again, five months after Yalta, at Potsdam near Berlin. The British and Americans had suffered from dramatic changes in their leadership. President Roosevelt had died suddenly in April. His place was taken by Harry Truman. And, part-way through the conference, Churchill was replaced by his rival Clement Attlee. Attlee's Labour Party had won the British general election. There were thus two new western leaders on the scene, neither having the wide experience of the men they replaced.

The Yalta decisions were confirmed, with some extra details. But it became clear that on some subjects there was a gulf between the USSR and the two Western Allies.
1 *Reparations.* Each power was to collect goods and equipment from its zone of Germany to compensate for its war losses. But the Soviet zone was chiefly agricultural: the major

industrial areas were all in the west. It was therefore arranged that the USSR should receive factory and transport equipment from the western zones as well. The details of how this would operate were unclear.

2 *Poland.* With Soviet encouragement the Poles had moved their border westwards, taking over two ancient provinces of Germany: Pomerania and Silesia. The Western powers disagreed strongly with this. In the face of Soviet determination, they could only leave the matter to the peace conference to settle. They were not to know that east-west disagreements would prevent the German peace conference taking place. The Poles, backed by the Red Army, remained in occupation.

The Atom Bomb: a New Factor in International Affairs

Though the war had ended in Europe, Japan continued to fight, and it seemed that the war in the Pacific would be ended only after the fiercest struggle, and at the cost of many thousands of lives. The Soviets prepared to join the Western Allies in the final assaults which were intended to end Japanese resistance. Meanwhile, at Potsdam, President Truman informed Stalin that a new type of bomb had been invented.

In August 1945 the war took a sudden, dramatic turn. On the 6th the Americans dropped an atomic bomb on the Japanese city of Hiroshima. The USSR carried out its promised attack on Japan on the 9th. Also on the 9th a second atomic bomb was dropped, this time on Nagasaki. Vast areas of Nagasaki and Hiroshima were destroyed, and about 110,000 people killed. It was a tragedy without parallel, and it brought the war to an abrupt end. The Allies had achieved their aim — the unconditional surrender of all their foes. It remained to be seen whether they could remain sufficiently united to rebuild their shattered world.

The atomic bomb not only ended the war, but also poisoned relations between the USSR and the two Western Allies, America and Britain. The latter refused to share the secrets of atomic power, and the USSR claimed this was contrary to the wartime agreements between them. They began an urgent programme to develop their own atomic weapons.

9

Spies of the Cold War: 1 Igor Gouzenko

The Second World War had been over only a matter of
weeks when events took place in Canada which were to have
great impact in the West. They happened in Ottawa, and
involved the Soviet embassy there.

The Code Expert Whom No One Would Believe

Igor Gouzenko was a cipher clerk at the Soviet embassy in
Ottawa. He held the rank of lieutenant in the Red Army. His
chief, Zabotin, was the head of a spy-ring in Canada which
sent vital secrets back to Moscow. Lieutenant Gouzenko
knew a good deal about this, since it was his job to encode
and decode many of the messages which went out or came in
over the embassy radio. He knew that the spy-ring in Canada
included officers in the Canadian armed forces, civil servants, and scientists. Some of the members were or had been
members of the Canadian Communist Party. In his two
years at the embassy, starting in 1943, Gouzenko sent off to
Moscow information about war production in Canada, including new guns, new explosives and developments in
radar. Some of the messages concerned Canadian, American
and British defence plans, and some dealt with Canadian
politics. More important still, although Gouzenko could not
recognise its full significance, some of the material he passed
to the USSR was concerned with the atomic bomb — then a
top-secret project.

Gouzenko and his family liked life in Canada, where they
were treated kindly. Life in the West, the Gouzenkos found,
was not at all as their education back in the USSR had
portrayed it. In August 1945 they decided not to heed an
order to return to Moscow. To show goodwill towards
Canada, Gouzenko decided to hand over to the Canadian
government enough material to cripple the spy-ring. On 5
September, 1945, Gouzenko took from his office the most
secret files he could find, and locked the door behind him for
the last time. He took the files to the *Ottawa Journal*, a well-
respected local newspaper. The staff did not know what to
make of him and sent him away, thus missing the biggest
scoop ever to come their way. Gouzenko went next to the

Ministry of Justice, and then to the Royal Canadian Mounted Police. He could not convince anyone of the importance of his story, or of the documents.

Meanwhile, as the hours passed, Soviet embassy staff had become thoroughly alarmed, and broke into his flat to search it. For a while the frightened Gouzenkos were sheltered by a kind neighbour. Igor was at his wits' end, not knowing how to make the Canadians take him seriously.

It was the attitude of the embassy staff, and their obviously frantic efforts to trace Gouzenko, which finally made the Canadian authorities act. Their experts quickly uncovered the amazing truth: spies working for the USSR had stolen vital secrets affecting Canada, the USA and Britain. All this had been organised through the embassy.

A Shock for the Western World

The full story was eventually published in February 1946, when thirteen spies were arrested. They included the British atom scientist Nunn May, who was arrested in London and confessed all his activities. The details were carried in every Western newspaper, and it was plain that the traitors had betrayed their countries and their fellow-citizens for one main reason: they were communists, and admired the USSR. The Gouzenkos settled in Canada.

The Gouzenko case had a profound effect on Western public opinion. It revealed the extent of just one Soviet spy cell—and obviously there were likely to be many others. It made it clear that communists, secret or admitted, might well be recruited as spies. It was one of the reasons why the widespread affection and admiration for the USSR cooled rapidly in the period immediately after the end of the Second World War. Western intelligence services were alerted to the fact of Soviet penetration of many vital secret organisations. The US army, for example, barred communists from holding posts where they would be concerned with secrets such as radar, atomic energy, or decoding. The 'spy war', in which East and West tried to gain knowledge of one another's industrial and defence secrets, was off to a fine start. The Gouzenko affair was to be followed by many others.

11

2 East-West Disagreement, 1945–1947

The Western Allies and the USSR No Longer Share a Common Aim

The 'Big Three'—the USA, Britain and the USSR—had managed to remain united only because of the overwhelming need to defeat a terrible enemy—Hitler's Germany. They had this one great aim in common. Once this had been achieved, the aims of the USSR and her Allies were no longer identical. The differences were to break up the wartime comradeship.

Different Aims in Eastern Europe

Stalin was determined, after 1945, that the countries of eastern Europe should have governments friendly to the USSR. The Western powers wanted free elections, as in their own countries, to be held in these states. But in 1945 the Red Army controlled these countries, and by 1948 communist parties had silenced all rivals throughout Poland, Hungary, Bulgaria, Romania, Czechoslovakia and East Germany.

Different Aims for a Polish-German Border

The Soviets insisted on setting the Polish-German frontier further to the west than the Allies, or the Germans, wished. It was fixed at the line of the Oder and western Neisse rivers, thus taking parts of the rich provinces of Pomerania and Silesia from Germany. The German people of these areas were forced to leave their homes and move westwards. The Western Allies never accepted this boundary change.

Different Aims for Germany

The Allies disagreed too over the treatment of Germany after

Pre-war and post-war Poland. The Russians gained a large area of eastern Poland, and the Poles, with Russian assistance, occupied a large part of eastern Germany

the war. So deep were the differences between the USSR and the Western powers that no peace treaty could ever be signed with Germany. The country's division continued.

Attitudes towards Germany were affected by the experiences each of the major powers had undergone:

The French had been defeated and occupied.

The British had exhausted their industry, seen their major cities bombed, and had used up all their wealth.

The Americans had made a stupendous industrial effort, had put enormous armies and fleets into action, and had supported their allies with floods of equipment.

The Soviets, however, in human terms had suffered more than anyone else. Hundreds of their cities had been devastated, and over 20,000,000 people killed — many more than in the Western powers put together. For every German division engaged by the Western armies, the Soviets had had to meet three.

In 1945 it was not surprising that the Soviets took a 'hard line' towards Germany, both in terms of reparations and the form of any future German government.

Lend-lease and Loans

Since 1941 the USA had supplied vast amounts of aid to her allies under the Lend-lease Act. By 1945 both Britain and the USSR were partly dependent on this help, which consisted not only of arms and munitions but of tools, food and

13

The human price of war in the USSR. Returning villagers, in the wake of the German retreat, look for their relatives among slaughtered civilians

raw materials. In May 1945 the US suddenly halted the lend-lease shipments. Although President Truman reversed this decision shortly afterwards, the Americans cut down supplies to the USSR, supplying only what they thought was essential for the Soviets' forthcoming attack on Japan. The Soviets resented this bitterly.

In January 1945 the US refused a Soviet request for a loan of six billion dollars. Another request, later that year, was simply 'lost' in Washington. The US government made it clear that loans would be made only if the Soviets would allow American investment and trade, on normal terms, in eastern Europe. The response from Stalin was furious, and the Soviets started their post-war re-building determined to rely only on their own resources.

East v. West in Iran

Iran, on the southern border of the Soviet Union, had been occupied by Soviet, British and American troops during the war, so that vital war supplies from the west could be sent to the USSR via the Iran railways. At the end of the war the Russians refused to withdraw their troops, demanding a share in the oil from the north Iranian oilfields. They pointed out that the British were already taking large amounts of oil from the fields in south Iran.

The Iranians made an agreement with the USSR that the latter should have a 51 per cent share in the oil from north Iran. Soviet troops then withdrew, in May 1946. But in 1947 the Iranian parliament cancelled the oil agreement, ignoring Soviet protests. In the following years Western influence in Iran appeared to be supreme: not only did the British continue to take their oil, but as one historian said, 'the Americans moved in — not with troops and revolution — but silently with dollars'. The Shah was very pro-Western; and Iranian cities looked more and more like those of the West, with American-style advertisements, cinemas and night-clubs.

Soviet pressures on Iran in 1945–46 seemed to Americans like proof of Soviet aggression. The growth of American commerce in Iran from 1947 onwards made the Soviet leaders feel they were being encircled by American power. In the years which followed, 'Russia fought tooth and nail to close her satellite nations to the "Iranian method"'. She was determined that Western influences and ideas should not triumph elsewhere as they had in Iran.

What Caused the Cold War?

The different policies followed by East and West in 1945–1946 were serious, and caused some sharp clashes. The genuine friendship of wartime began to cool. But those differences alone need not have produced the real bitterness and dangers of the Cold War, which started in earnest in 1947–1948. In those years the USA put forward its Marshall Plan for European recovery, and the Russians blockaded West Berlin. The Marshall Plan was rejected and denounced by the USSR; and the blockade of Berlin produced a mood both of alarm and determination in the West. But it is clear that the roots of the Cold War go back further than this. Some of the causes of the Cold War are these:

The 'Inevitable Clash' of Capitalism and Communism

The USSR had a very different form of government from the USA and the countries of western Europe. In the USSR, only

15

the Communist Party could exist. Most industry and agriculture was state-controlled. In the West there was political freedom, many parties existed, and most industry and agriculture was privately owned.

The Soviet leaders, and all communists, claimed and believed that their system was superior. For them, Karl Marx, writing in the nineteenth century, had discovered the laws of history. Marxism, as explained and developed by the great Soviet leader Lenin, showed plainly that the capitalist states of the West were at an earlier, inferior stage of development. Capitalism would collapse and be replaced, as had happened in the USSR. According to this 'Marxist-Leninist' view, the West was ripe for great changes. These changes would come about through internal weakness, revolution and war. A final great clash between the two systems was inevitable.

Communist parties everywhere in the West thus sought the overturning of the whole social system of their native lands. They looked to the USSR, 'the first Socialist country', for inspiration and direction. They were prepared to deny a completely free choice to others.

The most frequent accusation made against communism was that it was 'totalitarian'. This meant that it allowed no rivals. It held power by control of police and army, and by placing communists everywhere in key positions. It also used censorship to control what people were allowed to know, and directed education to control what they could be taught. Then, too, communists were contemptuous of religion. At times Russian churches had been suppressed, at others merely discouraged. All this was alien to the way of life in the West. The Western countries owed a good deal to their long Christian history; and their people had fought hard for freedom in politics, in education, and in the press. Most Western leaders therefore detested communism, and were anxious that it should not prevail.

The Suspicions of Eastern and Western Leaders

Western politicians had for years criticised the communist government of the USSR. Churchill, for example, said of

Lenin and Trotsky that they had 'driven man from the civilisation of the twentieth century into a condition of barbarism worse than the Stone Age...'. The Americans had actually refused to recognise the Soviet government till 1933.

The Soviet attitude to the West was yet more extreme. Stalin showed the most profound distrust of Western actions, even during the war years 1941–5, when the Western powers were his allies. To him, the USA was the home of capitalism, where workers were exploited in the interests of business profits. In 1947 he saw the generosity of the Marshall Plan simply as an effort to extend American business interests throughout Europe, including the USSR.

The Memory of the 'Intervention', and of Soviet Losses after the First World War

In 1918 and 1919 the Western states sent forces to Russia. The intention, at first, was to keep Russia in the war against Germany. But after the end of the First World War in November 1918 their troops and munitions were used to support the 'Whites' in their struggle against the communist government in Moscow. This intervention in the Russian Civil War was at best a confused and muddled affair, and

The intervention: Allied troops, from Czechoslovakia, Japan and Britain, in Vladisvostock, in the far east of the USSR; 1918

the Western soldiers were all to be withdrawn by October 1919. But the memory of this action stayed with the Russians, and left a legacy of intense bitterness. Soviet history books portray it as a full scale attempt to crush the communist state at birth, which was foiled by the Red Army. It was easy for the Soviet leaders to claim that the USSR was still under threat of attack from the West. The Soviet leaders were also conscious that their country had lost large areas to the east European states after the First World War. These included the undeniably Russian territory which had become part of eastern Poland. As early as 1943 Stalin revealed his wish to recover these lands.

Stalin: One of the Dictators

The people of the Western democracies were distrustful of dictatorships, of any type. Most people made little distinction between dictators like Hitler and Mussolini, who were fascists, and Stalin, a communist.

There was indeed much in Stalin's record which reinforced this view. He had, by his policies, been responsible for the murder of millions of Russian peasants in the early thirties. Many thousands of Red Army officers and Communist Party members had been 'purged' between 1935 and 1938. Such trials as were allowed were carefully staged, and were a mockery of justice. And in 1939 Stalin had made a pact with Hitler — the Soviet-German Non-aggression Pact. Under it Germany and the USSR had divided Poland between them.

After the Second World War Stalin's personal power was even greater. Communists in the USSR and eastern Europe praised him in ridiculous, extravagant terms. Gomulka, the Polish leader, said for example that Stalin was: 'an expert in everything, knew everything, decided everything, ran everything . . . the wisest of men'. To Western ears this sort of toadying was obnoxious, and the hallmark of the absolute dictator who ruled by fear. Stalin's great power, and the way he used it, was one of the obstacles to better understanding with the West.

Some of the underlying causes of the Cold War, however, were both deeper and older than the twentieth century. They will be considered in chapter 11.

'Ideas Men' of the Cold War: Kennan and Zhdanov

Kennan: a Russian Specialist in the US Foreign Service

George Kennan joined the American Foreign Service in 1926. In 1928 he became a specialist in Soviet affairs. He had plenty of opportunity to study the USSR, for he was an official in the US embassy at Riga, on the Baltic, which had been part of the Russian state till 1918. In 1933, when the USA recognised the USSR, he went to Moscow and helped to re-open an American embassy there.

Kennan liked Moscow, Soviet life and Russian literature. But he found the Soviet government under Stalin oppressive and murderous. In 1934 Kirov, leader of the Leningrad communists, was assassinated. It was the beginning of a black period in Soviet history. In a series of 'purges', many communists whom Stalin thought to be rivals, and many thousands of army officers, were executed. They even included the country's leading general, Tukhachevsky (June 1937). Kennan later said that to follow these trials, day by day, and report on them, was 'a sort of liberal education in the horrors of Stalinism'.

Kennan's Post-war Influence: his Telegram of February 1946

In 1946 the American government was baffled over its inability to cope with Soviet policies: particularly over eastern Europe, which was firmly in Soviet control. Kennan sent a long telegram from Moscow in February 1946, giving his explanation of the Soviet attitudes. The objects of Soviet leaders, he said, included the undermining of the Western powers, the hamstringing of Western defence, and the reduction of Western influence world-wide. The telegram was widely read by American political leaders, and it helped to shape their attitudes to the USSR.

The 'X' Article

In 1947 Kennan wrote an article which was published in the magazine *Foreign Affairs*. It was signed with an 'X' and it was called 'The Sources of Soviet Conduct'. He explained the dominance of the Communist Party, and how communists believed 'they alone knew what was good for society'. Moscow, he said, would always believe that 'the aims of the capitalist world are antagonistic to the Soviet regime'. Furthermore, Moscow would insist that it was always right: truth could not be found elsewhere.

But it was on foreign affairs that the X-article was to make the most impact. Kremlin policy, said Kennan,

'is a fluid stream which moves constantly, wherever it is permitted to move, toward a given goal. Its main concern is to fill every nook and cranny available to it in the basin of world power... The main thing is that there should always be pressure.'

To defeat this Soviet pressure Kennan advised the United States to adopt a policy of 'containment.' This meant opposing the USSR everywhere it might be necessary — not with bluster, but with patience and firmness. The USA must regard the Soviet Union 'as a rival, not a partner, in the political arena'.

Kennan's views, particularly the idea of containment, came to dominate thinking in Washington, and within a short time had been taken up by most ordinary Americans. He had a large part in shaping American attitudes to the USSR.

Zhdanov: an Extreme Marxist

Andrei Zhdanov was a thoroughly convinced, even fanatical Marxist. To him, the world must be seen as Marx had laid down. At home inside the USSR, everything must serve to advance the struggle of the working class. Abroad, capitalism must be opposed and eventually defeated.

Even before the Second World War, Zhdanov had become a sort of trouble-shooter for Stalin. He could be relied on for any task. He was ruthless, whether in forcing peasants to give up hoarded grain or in 'purging' the Leningrad communists of people thought to be unreliable. He was outstandingly successful as governor of Leningrad when the city was under siege after 1941. When the victory came in 1945 he was one of half-a-dozen men who might one day succeed Stalin.

Socialist Realism

In the 1930s Zhdanov had introduced the idea of 'Socialist Realism'. This meant that all art, sculpture, drama, literature and music had to 'serve the masses'. This meant that they had to be about ordinary workers, or about communist leaders; or they had to glorify labour and the business of building up socialism in the USSR. One of the results of this was that any art which was not readily understandable was condemned as rubbish. In 1946 Zhdanov directed a sharp attack on artists, poets, novelists and musicians who insisted on working according to their own feelings, rather than according to Socialist Realism. Well-known authors were expelled from the writers' union and found it impossible to publish their work. A popular comedian had his ration card withdrawn, and composers like Shostakovitch and Prokofiev had to change the sort of music they composed. The historian G. F. Alexander was disgraced and his *History of Western Philosophy* condemned because it was too kind to the West. Zhdanov also sponsored an absurd campaign which claimed practically every worthwhile invention to be Russian: radio, radar, steam engines— everything.

Zhdanov and Post War Policies

Zhdanov's advice is thought to lie behind Stalin's denunciation of Tito, the Yugoslav leader, in 1948. Tito's only crime was that he was determined to keep some independence from the USSR for Yugoslavia. It was Zhdanov's influence which led to Stalin's attempt to starve the West out of their zones of Berlin, in the same year (see p. 46).

Zhdanov at Warsaw: the Two Camps

Communist parties from east and west Europe sent representatives to Warsaw in September 1947. The meeting angrily denounced the Marshall Plan, and set up the Cominform (Communist Information Bureau). This was to link the

21

various communist parties in common action. Zhdanov made the main speech. It was a terrific blast against the West, foretelling another war.

'The changes caused by the war... have altered the political landscape of the world. The more the war recedes into the past, the more distinct are two great camps: the imperialist and anti-democratic camp, on the one hand; and the anti-imperialist and democratic camp, on the other. The main driving force of the imperialist camp is the USA. Allied with it are Britain and France. The main aim of the imperialist camp is to strengthen imperialism, to hatch a new imperialist war, to combat Socialism and democracy.'

Zhdanov's views were, of course, echoes of Stalin's. As Stalin's lieutenant, he helped to create the Cold War climate of 1947–8. He died suddenly in August 1948.

Churchill at Fulton: The 'Iron Curtain'

The Sinews of Peace

On a grey day in March 1946 Winston Churchill and President Truman arrived at Fulton, in the USA. Fulton was a small town, population about 8000, a few kilometres north of Jefferson City, Missouri. Churchill was to receive an honorary degree at Westminster College, where President Truman had once been a student. It had been announced beforehand that Churchill would also make a speech on world affairs. He had discussed this speech with Truman. Both men knew that it would help to change public opinion in the West towards the USSR. Churchill was no longer the British Prime Minister, having lost the general election of 1945, but his views still carried great weight.

The ceremony was held in the college gymnasium, packed with 3000 people. It was relayed to another 25,000 or so in the vicinity, and was also broadcast. Churchill called his address 'The Sinews of Peace'.

The old politician was in superb form. 'The name Westminster', he began, 'is somehow familiar to me. I seem to have heard it before.' His audience was instantly captured.

There was rapt attention as he continued. First, he described the state of the world: 'The awful ruin of Europe, with all its vanished glories, and of large parts of Asia, glares in our eyes.' He urged that the new United Nations Organisation should be given teeth, in the form of its own armed forces. He advised that the secrets of the atomic bomb, shared by the USA, Canada and Britain, should not be given to others, for the time being. Then he reached the crux of his message:

'the people of any country have the right and should have the power by constitutional action, by free unfettered elections with secret ballot, to choose or change the character or form of government under which they dwell.'

He was plainly referring here to eastern Europe, where the occupying Russians were supporting local communists in forcing their opponents out of politics (see Chapter 3).

Churchill went on to propose a continuing close alliance of Britain and her empire with the USA, in the interests of world peace. He warned of dangers threatening that peace: 'The Dark Ages may return, the Stone Age may return on the gleaming wings of science... Beware, I say; time may be short.'

The Iron Curtain

Churchill then made quite clear what he thought this threat to world peace was:

'A shadow has fallen upon the scenes so lately lighted by the Allied victory. Nobody knows what Soviet Russia and its Communist international organisation intends to do in the immediate future, or what are the limits, if any, to their expansive... tendencies.'

Churchill made it plain that he admired the Soviet people, and that he understood their need for secure western borders. However, he said,

'From Stettin on the Baltic to Trieste on the Adriatic an iron curtain has descended across the face of the Continent. Behind that line lie all the capitals of the ancient states of Central and Eastern Europe — Warsaw, Berlin, Prague,

Vienna, Budapest, Belgrade, Bucharest and Sofia. All these famous cities and the population around them lie in the Soviet sphere, and all are subject ... to control from Moscow.'

The communist parties of eastern Europe, said Churchill, though very small, had been given power 'far beyond their numbers', and were seeking total control. And even on the western side of the iron curtain freedom was menaced by communist parties working under orders from Moscow. They were 'a growing challenge and peril to Christian civilization'. He went on: 'I do not believe that Russia desires war. What they desire is the fruits of war, and the indefinite expansion of their power and doctrines.'

The Effects of the Iron Curtain Speech

In the West, the speech had a mixed reception. Many people found it hard to accept the picture of the USSR as a country bent on world conquest. Only gradually, over the next few years, did it begin to look as though Churchill might be right. But in Moscow the government papers reacted strongly, printing sections which seemed to indicate that an armed crusade against the USSR was about to start. 'Moscow received it hysterically' said one American reporter, 'as if the atomic bombs might start dropping before midnight.' Stalin accused Churchill of preparing a new war against the USSR.

Moscow and London Conferences, 1947

How Shall Germany be Governed?

There were two vital meetings of Foreign Ministers in 1947 —one in Moscow and one in London (March-April, and November-December). Some minor problems were cleared up. But the main subject was the enormous question: How is Germany to be governed in future? On this there was a furious clash. Molotov, the Soviet Minister, refused point-blank to consider anything but his own plan. This was for a central German government made up of 'anti-Fascist groups'. The western Ministers realised that Molotov's scheme would leave the whole of Germany ready for communist take-over.

They wanted a less centralised scheme, more like the pre-war Germany, but with completely free, democratic elections.

Bevin Encounters Molotov

Ernest Bevin, the British Minister at these conferences, had dealt with Russians and communists before. He knew that they would be tough, determined negotiators. At home, in the USSR, they had nothing to fear—there would be no press criticism if they failed to reach agreement. Western leaders, on the other hand, faced storms of comment in their parliaments and press. Even so, Bevin had hoped since 1945 that the British Labour government would be able to 'get on' with the Russians. He prolonged the negotiations, hoping for some compromise. He went to endless trouble in private talks with Molotov. His efforts were useless: the USSR wanted its own way in Germany, and would accept nothing else.

Christopher Mayhew was Bevin's Under-Secretary. He described the deadlock at the London meetings:

'I think the real disillusionment came with that Foreign Ministers' meeting in 1947. There they sat—Molotov, Bidault (France), Marshall (USA), Bevin—and Molotov much the cleverest of them I thought, and terribly skilful, terrible to listen to, frustrating, maddening. I remember Bevin coming away from one of these meetings: we went back to the Foreign Office with his senior officials and he slumped in his chair and he said "Can anyone tell me what to do? Can anyone tell me anything to do?"'

The conferences were utter failures. They mark the real end of the wartime alliance between the West and the Soviet Union.

The USSR at the United Nations
Blocking UN Action by Use of the Veto

The victorious Allies had set up the United Nations Organisation after the Second World War. The UNO would, it was hoped, preserve world peace. Members promised not to go to war. Disputes were to be settled in the UN, peacefully.

The Great Powers had been realistic about one feature of the UN. They decided that they must be unanimous before any strong action could be taken in the UN's Security Council. The right of veto — blocking any decision — was given to them.

Britain and the United States had both said they intended to pursue a foreign policy in accord with UN principles. But they quickly found in the post-war years that any UN action was repeatedly prevented by the USSR's veto. Again and again, dozens of times, the Soviets said 'No'. To the West it seemed that the new world organisation, of which so much was hoped, was being hamstrung by one nation. The Soviets were wrecking the UN. The Soviets, of course, saw things very differently. The United States and its allies had a permanent majority in all parts of the UN at that time. Use of the veto merely ensured that decisions were not taken against Soviet interests. The Security Council veto, said the Soviets, was being properly used, in line with the intentions of 1945.

The Veto Debate in the UN

The row about the Soviet veto blew up with a vengeance in September 1947. There was an excited, angry debate. General Marshall accused the Soviets of ruining the United Nations. Vyshinsky, representing the USSR, accused the USA of aggression, fascism and seeking to control the world. A journalist reported

'the Cold War between Russia and the United States is now several degrees warmer.

Andrei Vyshinsky's onslaught is regarded as a diatribe of lies, a monstrous smear on all Americans which is savagely resented.

There is now an Everest of anti-Russian feeling in the country — a mountain-range of suspicion, mistrust and anger...

Every word Vyshinsky spoke means another 1,000,000 dollars allotted to the Marshall Plan. *'

---

* For the Marshall Plan, see pages 42–4

3 Mid and Eastern Europe, 1945–1948

'The Lands Between'

The countries of eastern Europe were a focus of attention in the years 1945–50. They formed a broad belt across the continent, from the Baltic Sea in the north to the Black Sea and the Mediterranean in the south. They lay between the rich, industrialised states of western Europe and the rising, developing power of the communist USSR. The Soviets regarded them as important for their security. The West did not wish to see them dominated by the USSR, through their communist parties.

Poland, Czechoslovakia, Hungary, Romania, Bulgaria and Yugoslavia were all mainly agricultural. Peasants formed the greater part of the populations: as much as 80 per cent in the case of pre-war Bulgaria. In some places the land was held in small-holdings, but in others huge estates owned by nobles survived down to 1945. It is not surprising that there were 'peasant' political parties in all these countries. In any free elections, these peasant parties could always do well.

Between Germany and the USSR

The east European countries were weak. None of them could challenge Germany, on the western side, nor the USSR on the east. When in 1945 Germany lay in ruins and complete defeat, it was certain that eastern Europe would at the least be very strongly influenced by the one surviving Great Power of the area. In fact, there were powerful reasons why this influence was irresistible.

The Red Army in Eastern Europe

As the German forces had been thrust back from Russia, the

Red Army units in Prague, May 1945

Red Army had fought its way westward. It crossed the old Soviet borders, entering Poland and the other countries southward. In 1944 and 1945 the Red Army occupied the east European capitals and took control. Romania and Hungary were treated as enemies; they had been allies of the Germans. Yugoslavia was the only area where the Red Army's role was minor, for there Tito's partisan army played the greater part in ridding the country of German forces. Bulgaria too was something of an exception – though she had joined Germany in war against the West, she had not helped directly in the attack on the USSR. She had however supported the Germans in various other ways, and in September 1944 the USSR declared war on Bulgaria and occupied the country.

By May 1945, therefore, the Red Army controlled all the countries of eastern Europe, save only Greece, Albania and Yugoslavia.

The Role of the Communist Parties

Before 1939 the east European communist parties were very

28

weak. But in some areas, like Poland, communists played a major role in resisting the Germans. They took part in sabotage, the assassination of German officers, and guerilla warfare.

In 1944–5 these communist parties welcomed the Red Army. They were given Soviet support, and with this were able to exercise much greater influence over post-war politics than their mere numbers would have allowed. On top of this, all parties and groups which were even suspected of having been pro-German were eliminated or deprived of power in 1945. This helped to leave the field clear.

The 'Baggage-Train' Leaders

The advancing Red Army brought in its wake men and women who had long been communists but whose efforts had been mostly unsuccessful till then. Many of these exiled Czech, Polish, Romanian and other communists had spent all or part of the war in the USSR. Some, like the Romanian Anna Pauker, had broadcast to their homelands from Moscow. Some had been parachuted into their home countries to organise resistance to the Germans. All were reliable communists who would act on Moscow's instructions. In 1944–5 the Soviets sent these people home and gave them firm backing. They included:

> G. Dimitrov and V. Kolarov, who took up dominant posts in the 'Fatherland front' in Bulgaria;
> A. Pauker and V. Luca, who became members of the Romanian government;
> B. Bierut, S. Radkiewicz and H. Minc who took key positions in Poland;
> M. Rakosi, E. Gero and I. Nagy who were all to become Prime Ministers of Hungary;
> K. Gottwald and R. Slansky in Czechoslovakia. Gottwald was to become Prime Minister, aided by a 'Workers' militia' under Slansky's command.

A Period of Coalitions

At the end of the war, in 1945, the eastern states had

coalition governments in which communists and non-communists were supposed to work together. Some notable reforms were made—especially concerning land ownership. In Hungary, Poland and Czechoslovakia the last great medieval estates were broken up and transferred to the peasants. Peasant and Small Farmers' parties played their part in carrying out these coalition policies.

Slicing Salami

The coalitions were awkward alliances. With Soviet power to back them, the communists were impatient to seize full control. They wanted to move faster than even Stalin thought wise. Thus the communist Dimitrov made his party's intentions for Bulgaria plain in 1946. They wanted to create a 'People's Republic', i.e. a state where the Communist Party would be supreme.

'Bulgaria will be a People's Republic which will leave no open doors for a return to the shameful past of Monarchism, or Fascism...

Bulgaria will be a People's Republic, a free and sovereign country. It will not dance to the tune of different capitalist corporations and trusts which want to enslave small nations...

Bulgaria will be a People's Republic. It will not grease the axle of any anti-Slav or anti-Soviet policy.'

Soviet and communist pressure quickly forced many Liberal, Social Democrat or Peasant politicians to resign, or retire, or flee. At first there were some genuinely free elections, but this also changed. By late 1948 elections everywhere were either shamelessly rigged, or voters were simply given a choice between various communist supporters. Threats and intimidation reduced the different governments to puppets of Moscow. Opponents were arrested, often on the charge of 'Fascist sympathy'. Peasant leaders in Hungary and Poland fled abroad. In Hungary independent socialists who would not support the communist line were simply kept out of parliament. Others were imprisoned, or executed after faked trials.

Step by step, communist control was strengthened. The Hungarian communist leader Rakosi quite openly described the process as being 'like slicing off salami', piece by piece, till all his opponents were destroyed or powerless. By the summer of 1948 the communists everywhere had gained power. They did not intend to give it up. The independent peasant parties had all been eliminated, or turned into mere puppets.

A Trainload of Gifts for Stalin

The new governments of eastern Europe were modelled on the Soviet Union. One important way in which eastern Europe was 'Sovietised' was through the trades unions, which were under strong government control. This describes part of the process in Poland:

'Trades Unionists and delegations of Poles from all walks of life, from peasants to poets, went to the Soviet Union during 1949 to study "Soviet Experience". Festivals of Soviet arts and films, competitions for the best translations from the Russian, exhibitions of Soviet architecture, and other events occurred every month. A declaration of December 1948 had laid down that there was only one way of building Socialism. The party leadership now submitted the country to a crash course in Soviet socialism. Continuous manifestations of gratitude to the Soviet Union and its leadership were staged. The country celebrated Stalin's seventieth birthday on 21 December 1949 as if it were a national holiday. A special train loaded with gifts was despatched to Moscow.'

Czechoslovakia — from Popular Front to Communist Power

A Coalition Dominated by Communists

The 'coalition stage' in eastern European governments lasted longest in Czechoslovakia: till February 1948. Unlike other eastern countries, the Czechs knew what it meant to have a free parliament. Before 1938 they had enjoyed a measure of democracy as it was known in the West. They expected

31

elections to be completely free, with a variety of parties taking part. They had enjoyed a free press. From 1945–8, under their 'Popular Front' government, these freedoms remained more or less intact. In 1948 the communists were the largest single party. They were united and determined. A communist was in charge of the Interior Ministry, which controlled the police. The democrat parties, if they could have combined, were numerically stronger. But they were hopelessly divided. Through the communists, Russian influence was irresistible, and in 1947 Stalin forbad the Czechs to take part in the American Marshall Plan. It would have brought much-needed aid to the country, and the democrat Foreign Minister, Jan Masaryk, remarked sadly 'We have become mere vassals'. Masaryk was a friend of the West.

Prague, February 1948

In February 1948 the communist Interior Minister dismissed eight senior officers in his police, replacing them with reliable, pro-communist ones. The democratic parties protested, and their ministers resigned from the coalition, hoping to bring down the government. The communists then took ruthless action. Armed groups walked into radio and newspaper offices and took control. The headquarters of the other political parties were occupied, thus paralysing them. Thousands of communist workers, all in blue overalls with guns stuck through the belts, paraded in the streets. Student protests against these events were quelled by police gunfire. And the Soviets sent to Prague their Deputy Foreign Minister to watch over the situation. The aged president of the country, under great pressure, agreed to form a new government 'without reactionaries'. This turned out to be one of communists and their supporters alone. The coalition period was over.

After the Prague Coup

Almost without bloodshed, the communists had taken control of the country. On 10 March Masaryk's body was found in the courtyard of his Foreign Ministry building. He had

The show of force in Prague by the communist-controlled police and militia groups from Czech factories. March 1948

either been pushed from his office window, or had perhaps thrown himself out in despair.

The communist coup was followed by a series of purges. Non-communists were removed from power everywhere — in the armed forces, in the civil service, in education, local government and even in youth organisations. The defeated democratic parties were kept in being in name only. They were packed with reliable stooges who could be relied on to vote as the communists wished.

The West was appalled at the end of Czech democracy and at the sheer ruthlessness of the communist takeover. It seemed possible that France and Italy might be next on the list. Both had strong communist parties.

The Closing of Eastern Europe

During 1947 and 1948, as communist control tightened, the states of eastern Europe were closed to the West. Tourism, which had revived after 1945, was stopped. All contact with the west was made difficult. Even within the communist bloc, it became almost impossible to cross frontiers, except for delegations of officials, or parties of trade unionists. Visits to the USSR were not available to private citizens in the West. There were probably two reasons for this defensive policy. One was that there was an enormous amount of re-building to be done, particularly in the USSR and Poland. For hundreds of kilometres in European Russia there was not a house or even a telegraph pole left standing after the German retreat in 1944. Reconstruction was a gigantic task, for which the Soviets wanted privacy. They were taking vast quantities of goods from eastern Europe to assist their rebuilding. Their problems were also aggravated by famine in the Ukraine, and the horrific scale of this only began to be realised in the West some years later. Stalin did not wish the USSR's weakness, and its great problems, to be broadcast to the world. The second reason was that this period saw the changeover from the 'coalition' period in the East European countries. One-party states, with communist control at every level from government to trade union and youth league, were being firmly established. Stalin, again, wanted Western influences kept out at this important time.

By the summer of 1948 the Iron Curtain across Europe, of which Churchill had spoken two years before, had become obvious to everyone.

East Germany Becomes a People's Republic

East Germany, more than any other part of eastern Europe, was under the closest Soviet control after the end of the war in 1945. The USSR dismantled factories, and shipped out enormous amounts of machinery, coal and minerals.

In 1946 the popular Social Democrat Party was forced to merge with the much less popular Communist Party. Communist control in every region and city became absolute. Though a variety of other groups took part in local government, they were all communist-controlled.

In 1949, partly as a reply to the creation of a new West German state out of the western zones, east Germany was proclaimed an independent country to be known as the German Democratic Republic (GDR). In form the GDR was similar to the 'People's Republics' which had been set up in Poland, Bulgaria and elsewhere. In the following years the GDR proved itself the closest possible supporter of Russian policies in Europe.

Soviet and Western Attitudes to Events in Eastern Europe

Truman and Molotov expressed the different Western and Soviet attitudes to eastern Europe very clearly in 1948.

President Truman speaks to the US Congress in 1948

'Most countries of the world have joined together in the United Nations in an attempt to build a world order based on law and not on force ... One nation, however, has persistently obstructed the work of the UN by constant abuse of the veto. That nation has vetoed twenty-one proposals for action in a little over two years.

But that is not all. Since the close of hostilities the Soviet Union and its agents have destroyed the independence and democratic character of a whole series of nations in eastern Europe. It is this ruthless course of action, and the clear design to extend it to the remaining free nations of Europe, that have brought about the critical situation in Europe today. The tragic death of the Republic of Czechoslovakia has sent a shock throughout the civilised world. Now pressure is being brought to bear on Finland ... Greece is under direct military attack from rebels actively supported by her Communist dominated neighbours ... The methods vary but the pattern is all too clear.'

The Russian Foreign Minister, Molotov, replies to an American note in May 1948

'As regards relations between the USSR and its neighbours ... these relations have considerably improved since the war. This has found expression in treaties of friendship and

The Cold War

A West German view of the plight of eastern Europe. Poland, Czechoslovakia, Hungary, Romania and Bulgaria carry the banner 'Thank Our Liberators' under the watchful eye of the USSR

mutual assistance...treaties which are aimed exclusively against a repetition of aggression on the part of Germany.

The USA is also pursuing a policy of consolidating its relations with neighbouring countries, such as Canada and Mexico, as well as other American countries, which is perfectly understandable. It is equally understandable that the Soviet Union is also pursuing a policy of consolidating its relations with neighbouring countries of Europe.

As regards the countries of eastern Europe, it is known that since the war important democratic transformations have taken place there... It would be utterly wrong to ascribe the democratic transformations which have taken place there to the intervention of the Soviet Union in the domestic affairs of these countries. The promotion of Communists to leading positions is perfectly natural, because the peoples of those countries regard the Communists as the most consistent fighters against a new war.'

The Special Case of Yugoslavia

The Success of the Partisan Army under Tito

In 1944 the Red Army had entered Yugoslavia. But even so, the country was largely freed by a Yugoslav army: the communist partisan army of Marshal Tito. It was partly equipped with munitions supplied by the British from their Middle East and Italian airfields, as well as with supplies captured from Italians. By May 1945, after three years of desperate and bitter struggles, this partisan army had cleared most of the country of German forces.

Tito had spent much time in Moscow, and was a devoted communist. But he was also fiercely patriotic. He had obtained an agreement from the Soviets that the Red Army would stay in Yugoslavia only temporarily.

Tito and the Post War Coalition Government

At first, as in other east European states, a coalition government was set up. It included Royalist and Social Democrat members. But Tito, who was Prime Minister, saw this as an irritating, temporary affair. He wanted complete communist control — a 'People's Republic,' in communist language. He later said

'The unified government which had been set up on 8 March 1945, on outside advice, was not...suited in all aspects to the existing state of affairs in Yugoslavia. It was only a transition period...And in that period our opponents at home and abroad still had illusions about "who is going to get the better of whom". But we suffered from no illusions. We knew exactly how the whole affair would end, namely in the defeat of our opponents...we knew that cooperation could not last long.'

He went on to explain how his chief political opponents, under pressure, left his government. The communists then had the complete power they had planned for. Large farms and estates were broken up, and given to the peasants. 'The land belongs to those who cultivate it', said the country's new constitution. Industries were nationalised. 'Now,' said

37

Tito, 'we are in possession of the basic elements for building Socialism in our country.'

The Break with Stalin's Russia

In 1948 an open quarrel broke out between the Soviets and the Yugoslav communists. The immediate causes were trivial. Tito would not be treated as an underling. He refused to speak of the USSR in the fulsome, glowing terms which were usual in all the other communist parties. He objected fiercely when the Soviets recruited spies in Yugoslavia. And, above all, the Yugoslavs insisted that they owed their freedom to their own partisan army, rather than to the Red Army.

The quarrel grew, splitting Yugoslavia from the east European bloc of states, and from the USSR. Stalin called Tito a traitor, and an agent of western imperialism. 'I shall shake my little finger,' he is supposed to have said, 'and there will be no Tito.' He stopped all Soviet economic aid to Yugoslavia, and withdrew Soviet specialists and advisers. It was all in vain: the Yugoslav communists went their own way, determined not to be dominated by Stalin or the USSR.

Yugoslavia Keeps its Independence

Yugoslavia badly needed industrial and technical help to rebuild after the wartime losses and neglect. Tito sought help from the West. In Yugoslavia a new type of government was gradually developed — still communist, but allowing more personal freedom than in other eastern states. Tito kept the country neutral. In 1955 it did not join the Warsaw Pact which bound the USSR and the east European States in a military alliance. Though the USSR was later to apologise for its treatment of the Yugoslavs, the breach was never healed. In 1968, for example, when the Soviet invasion of Czechoslovakia was endorsed by all the other east European governments, Tito denounced it firmly.

Tito and his colleagues succeeded in breaking away from the powerful influence of the USSR. 'Our revolution', he said, 'was specific. And our road to socialism is specific too.' He meant that it was not the Soviet road.

4 The Emergence of the Two Power-blocs, 1947–1953

The Truman Doctrine: Helping Others to Resist Communism

A Weakened and Subdued Europe

In the spring of 1947 Europe's situation seemed pitiable:

1 Western Europe was war-shattered and weak. A bitter, prolonged winter had brought blizzards and fuel crises.
2 Eastern Europe was Soviet-dominated. Communists had taken power almost everywhere, though most people did not support them. Opponents had been forced out of politics, terrified by threats, imprisoned or murdered.
3 Communist guerillas were fighting to take control in Greece, though they had been rejected in elections there. Stalin had demanded that the USSR be given a naval and military base in Greece. He wanted Alexandroupolis, on the Aegean Sea, for this.
4 Turkey was under Soviet pressure. Stalin had demanded a permanent base in the vital Turkish narrows which led from the Black Sea to the Mediterranean. He had revived the USSR's claim to the areas of Kars, Ardahan and Artvin, which had been ceded to Turkey in 1918. Soviet troops had concentrated on the Turkish border.

The British supported both Turkish and Greek governments with money and had an army of 40,000 men in Greece. Its presence prevented the communist guerillas from taking over. But in February 1947 Britain told the US that she could no longer afford this support to Greece and Turkey. She would have to pull out.

Truman's Message to Congress: March 1947

In 1945 and 1946 the Americans had largely withdrawn from Europe. Their large armies had been taken quickly back across the Atlantic and demobilised. Only small occupation forces remained, in Germany. It seemed as though the USA was leaving Europe to herself, just as she had done in 1918. But things were about to change.

The President and his Secretary of State, General Marshall, carefully prepared the way for a new era in American policies. They explained to influential senators that both Turkey and Greece might fall to communism if the US did not take over the British role. It meant a large programme of aid. Senator Vandenberg, whose support was essential because of his great influence in the Republican Party, was won over. 'Mr President', he said, 'if that's what you want there's only one way to get it. That is to make a personal appearance before Congress and scare hell out of the country.'

Truman delivered the vital speech to Congress on 12 March, 1947. He made the dire situation absolutely clear.

'The United States has received from the Greek government an urgent appeal for financial and economic assistance... The very existence of the Greek State is today threatened by the terrorist activities of several thousand armed men, led by communists... The United States must supply this assistance...

No government is perfect... The government of Greece is not perfect. Nevertheless it represents 85 per cent of the members of the Greek parliament, who were chosen in an election last year. Foreign observers, including 692 Americans, considered this election to be a fair expression of the views of the Greek people.'

Truman explained that Turkey had asked for similar aid, and condemned the Soviet pressure on the Turks. In his opinion, the world was faced with two completely opposed 'ways of life'. The first included free elections, freedom of speech, and freedom of religion. But, said Truman,

'The second way of life is based upon the will of the minority forcibly imposed upon the majority. It relies upon terror and

40

The Truman doctrine was quickly put into practice. One year after Truman's message to Congress the Turkish ship *Yazgat* is loaded with American tanks in New York. April 1948

oppression, a controlled press and radio, fixed elections, and the suppression of personal freedom.'

Truman then put forward what came to be known as the 'Truman Doctrine':

'It must be the policy of the United States to support free peoples who are resisting attempted subjugation by armed minorities or by outside pressures.'

Whilst Congress debated the President's request for $400,000,000 to aid the two countries the fate of Greece hung in the balance. The first moves were made in the communist-controlled areas to set up a 'People's Republic'. However, British troops were not withdrawn immediately, and American naval vessels appeared at Greek ports. American economic aid began to assist the Greek government. The communist groups were checked, then defeated. Two and a half years later they gave up the struggle. The Truman Doctrine had gained its first victory.

41

The European Recovery Programme, or 'Marshall Plan'

Marshall at Harvard, 5 June 1947

If Europe was to be restored to prosperity and strength it needed yet more help from the United States. Far-sighted American politicians and officials put up the idea that the European nations should receive long-term aid to enable them to re-equip their industries and improve their agriculture and commerce. George Kennan, Dean Acheson and Senator Vandenberg all had a part in this idea. By this time Kennan was regarded as the US's chief expert on Soviet matters; Acheson was an Under-Secretary of State, very influential in foreign affairs; and Vandenberg headed the Republican Party's Foreign Affairs Committee. The scheme was put in the form of an invitation by General Marshall, speaking at Harvard University. He suggested that the European nations together make a plan to accept and use American help. The offer, he said, was not directed against any country, but 'against hunger, poverty, desperation and chaos'.

Bevin's Response to the Marshall Invitation

Britain's Labour Foreign Minister, Ernest Bevin, heard extracts from Marshall's speech early next morning, on BBC radio. 'As I listened, tears came to my eyes', he said later. 'For the first time I saw a ray of hope for Europe.' He went quickly to his Foreign Office headquarters, only to find that he was too early for his staff. When they finally arrived they studied the Harvard speech with great care. Bevin acted rapidly – his officials were on their way to Paris that very afternoon, to begin the European response.

Seventeen European states benefited from the Marshall Plan. They received loans, or goods, or gifts, to the value of 13 billion dollars between 1948 and 1952. The USSR came to the first discussions, but then walked out, saying that the plan was simply a way for the USA to dominate Europe economically. The Russians prevented the East European nations from joining, though at least two—Czechoslovakia and Poland—wished to take part.

The USSR and the Marshall Plan

The British *Daily Mail* of 3 July 1947 reported on the Paris meetings at which the Marshall offer was discussed:

'MOLOTOV RINGS DOWN THE IRON CURTAIN

Bevin: We've Faced Threats Before

From Wilson Broadbent, Diplomatic Correspondent

Paris, Wednesday

Soviet Russia has finally refused to cooperate with Britain and France on the Marshall Plan for rebuilding Europe. If words mean anything, Mr Molotov has also tonight rung down the Iron Curtain with a resounding clang.

Even the few loopholes which remain for trade and economic cooperation between East and West will be closed if Mr Molotov's attitude here is confirmed in Moscow.'

The Daily Mail was quite clear about where the blame should lie:

'If, therefore, in years to come, anybody is sufficiently interested to ask who created the Western bloc, the answer must be Mr Molotov, in Paris, in the early days of July 1947.'

Bevin could be quite as firm as Molotov. He finally 'blew up' at the Paris meetings. He had at last decided that it was beyond anyone to 'get on' with the USSR:

'Mr Bevin was outspoken. He described Mr Molotov's remarks as being based on a complete travesty and misrepresentation of everything the British government had submitted to the meetings. He supposed that the method was to go on repeating these misrepresentations in the hope that somebody would at last believe them.'

The Success of Marshall Aid

The plan was remarkably successful; the states of western Europe rebuilt their economies, increased their production and saw their standards of living rise. The Americans provided not only cash and credits, but machinery, vehicles, petrol, coal, cotton and steel, besides foods of various kinds. Some American politicians opposed the plan; but their opposition dissolved when news of the communist takeover in Czechoslovakia was received in February 1948.

The Motives behind the Marshall Plan

The American aim in providing such vast sums of aid was partly economic: they wanted a prosperous Europe which would buy American goods, and their own 'dollar crisis' would be helped if the Europeans could sell goods to them in return. The plan laid down that the European countries would keep the value of their currencies steady, and work towards freer international trade.

The plan was also political: a prosperous Europe, with strong democratic governments, would be more likely to resist communism. The Americans almost certainly knew that the USSR, with its hostility towards capitalism, would not be able to take part. The USSR wanted the aid, but not if it meant revealing its post-war weaknesses. And even if the Soviets had not withdrawn, the American Congress would have been unlikely to pass the plan if the Soviet Union had been included.

Even when these aspects of the plan are considered, it remains an act of generosity. Churchill called the Marshall aid programme 'the most unsordid act in history'.

Marshall Aid and the Cold War

The Soviet leaders had hoped to profit from the divided and broken state of Europe. They tried in 1948 to produce an eastern counterpart to the Marshall Plan for the states they controlled behind the 'Iron Curtain'. This they called the Molotov Plan. But their resources were no match for those of the USA, and recovery in the east was much slower. The Marshall Plan and the Soviet reaction to it therefore helped to make the division of Europe permanent.

In one important respect the plan marked a great change in American attitudes. The USA was clearly not going to turn her back on European affairs.

The Problems of Divided Germany

The Partition of Germany

Germany had been divided between the four powers in the summer of 1945 (see p. 5). There were Soviet, American, British and French zones, each controlled by a high-ranking officer and a large staff. Berlin, too, was divided, each of the Allies being responsible for its own sector of the capital.

None of the four powers intended that Germany should remain divided. They wished to treat it as a single country. They meant, eventually, to sign a peace treaty with this new, post-war Germany. But a whole series of vital matters were seen very differently by the Western Allies, on the one hand, and the USSR on the other.

1 Germany's Eastern Frontier with Poland

In 1945 The Soviets had handed over to the Poles the German provinces of Silesia and Pomerania. At the Yalta Conference in February 1945 Roosevelt and Churchill, for the United States and Britain, had accepted this only as a temporary arrangement, to be adjusted later. The USSR and Poland, however, treated the matter as finally settled.

2 Reparations

By 1946 the Russians were known to be taking from their zone of Germany immense amounts of industrial plant and machinery — more than even the disputed Yalta figure would have allowed. They were also taking large quantities of finished, manufactured goods — which the Yalta agreement forbad. They also sealed off their zone from any trade with the West, so that the Western Allies had to import vast amounts of food and other goods to maintain their zones. Dissatisfied with the Soviet actions, and alarmed by the immense drain on their own resources, the Western powers stopped reparations deliveries to the East in May 1946.

3 Berlin

The city of Berlin was over a hundred kilometres inside the

Soviet zone. Its council offices, university and main power-stations were all inside the Soviet sector, and were Soviet-controlled. The city's first council elections in the autumn of 1946 were a crushing defeat for the communist-controlled Social Unity Party in all three western sectors. In the Soviet sector the elections were 'rigged' so that the communists gained a ludicrously large majority. The USSR set up a communist city government in East Berlin; the West responded by establishing both a new council and a new university for West Berlin.

4 New Currencies in Germany

To deal with the problem of inflation a new German currency was urgently needed. No agreement could be reached between the three Western powers and the USSR. The West introduced its new 'westmarks' in their zones, saying this was essential for the health of the economy. On 23 June 1948 the Soviets introduced their new currency, which they wished to make legal throughout all Germany, including Berlin. The West retaliated by introducing the westmarks to Berlin. The two currencies circulated together in Berlin, and the value of the eastern mark quickly fell to a fraction of the westmark. Clearly, Berliners wished to hold and use the western currency, and they had little confidence in the eastern one.

Even before the westmark had been issued in Berlin the USSR had begun to interfere with traffic between the city and the western zones. Traffic on the autobahns from the west was halted and delayed as early as the end of March 1948. Trains were held up for prolonged inspections. Finally, on 24 June, the day after the westmark had appeared in Berlin, the Soviet forces stopped all road, rail and water traffic. West Berlin appeared to be cut off from the western zones of Germany, and indeed from western Europe. It was a western island, surrounded by Soviet armies. Soviet spokemen claimed that the West had no right in Berlin. The Soviet commander asserted that his troops controlled not only the land routes to Berlin, but the air routes as well. All the cards seemed to be in Soviet hands; the blockade appeared unbreakable.

The Berlin Air Lift

A Difficult Decision for the Western Allies

The Western powers had arrived at a crisis point, and faced a terrible decision. If they gave in to the Soviet pressure Berlin would be communist-dominated, and perhaps, before long, the rest of Germany too. General Lucius Clay, the American Military Governor in Germany, wanted to use an armoured column to force a way through along an autobahn. But the three powers decided instead to try to supply West Berlin by air. This would avoid a possible clash with Soviet troops. Even so, the world knew that the war-time alliance with the USSR had finally split. The clash over Berlin might easily lead to a new war — this time against the USSR.

An 'Air Bridge' to Berlin: is it Possible?

To supply West Berlin every available plane — American and British, military and commercial — would be needed. The British would organise the flights from their zone of the

Eastern and Western views of the Berlin blockade. Left: The Airlift steps easily over the ring of Soviet soldiers (a cartoon from West Germany). Right: The Western Allies are caught in the Berlin sack (a cartoon from the USSR)

47

country, and the Americans from theirs, but about two-thirds of the crews and planes would be American. The French said they could not help with planes, but would assist in other ways, including the construction of a new airstrip in their sector of Berlin, at Tegel. But no one knew whether the airlift could succeed in keeping Berlin supplied. No one knew how long it would have to continue, and a winter lay ahead. In addition, there were hundreds of new problems to be solved. How were the masses of aircraft to be controlled, on the ground and at the loading areas? The Western Allies had the right to use certain 'air corridors' across East Germany to Berlin. But these corridors were limited in width, and no one knew whether they would be adequate for the hundreds of aircraft which would have to use them. How could heavy equipment be transported by air? Was it possible to carry sufficient coal to keep West Berlin's factories working? Was it more economic to fill planes with loaves of bread, or with the flour from which bread could be made?

Confrontation: East v. West in Germany

One thing was quite clear: the struggle for Berlin was on, and with it the struggle for the hearts and minds of the German people, who watched anxiously to see how well the West would stand up to the Soviet pressures. Neither side was ready to give way. With British agreement, the Americans moved two squadrons of giant B-29 bombers to bases in Britain. From those bases, they could if necessary reach the USSR; and they were equipped to carry atomic bombs.

'Operation Vittles' — Keep Berlin Supplied!
10 September 1948. Wunstorf airfield, near Hanover, British zone of Germany.

The roar of large transport planes never stops. They race down the runway at a rate of one every three minutes — Dakotas, Avro Yorks, Lancastrians. They wait in dozens on the tarmac for their turn to take off again, bound for Gatow airport, on the western side of Berlin.

The 'outward' cargo is unloaded. Then, some of the airfield's 3000 German workers shift the sacks of flour, the bags of coal, the canned foods, the medical supplies. Once inside the planes, the load has to be carefully stowed according to its weight. Jeeps buzz around the airfield, carrying the men who make the checks. The aircrews collect their new cargo lists and fill in records. Once airborne, the course is set to join dozens of others in the air corridor across East Germany. The streams of planes come in from RAF and Coastal Command stations all over the British zone.

About ninety minutes after take-off, the planes touch down in Berlin. They are directed to unloading positions, and the trucks are immediately backed up to receive the precious cargoes. Once emptied, the planes are swept clean of dust and litter by waiting teams of women. Unending streams of vehicles carry the supplies to distribution centres in the city. The planes fly out of Berlin down a different corridor. Here they are joined by yet more aircraft which have come in from the south, under American control. Many of these aircraft have been unloading at Berlin's great civil airport, Tempelhof. Once clear of Eastern Germany, the planes head back for their bases to begin yet another trip.

At the airfields in southern and western Germany new crews wait to take over the aircraft. The planes fly day and night, stopping only when servicing is due.

4000 Tonnes Per Day

West Berlin was kept supplied. The needed average of 4000 tonnes daily was reached, and passed. The coal went to the power stations and factories, and the food and flour were enough to keep up basic rations. Newsprint was brought in so that the newspapers could continue publishing. But the West Berliners had a cold winter during 1948–9, for none of the fuel brought in could be spared for private houses. The planes did not return from Berlin empty, for thousands of children were evacuated and there was a constant flow of wares, produced in the factories, to be sold in the West.

The airlift formed a new link of friendship between the Germans and the Western powers. It was clear that the USA, Britain and France were determined not to abandon

The Cold War

Berlin to domination by the USSR. One American aircrew made hundreds of friends among German children as they dropped showers of chocolate bars, attached to parachutes made from handkerchieves, on their approaches to Tempelhof. 'Der Schokoladenflieger' — the chocolate flyer — did more for German-US relationships than many a diplomat. On Christmas Day 1948 thousands of children welcomed a US Skymaster loaded with small gifts, and whose pilot was dressed in the familiar costume of Santa Claus.

The British and American planes made about 275,000 flights. They carried nearly two and a half million tonnes of fuel, food and vital materials. Although the USSR threatened to hold paratroop exercises in the vital air corridors, it was plain that it could not destroy the 'air bridge' built by the Allies. To do that it would have to shoot down the planes, and that it was not prepared to do. The Soviets lifted surface travel restrictions through East Germany to Berlin in May 1949, though the airlift continued for another four months. By then the Soviets had installed their own communist mayor in East Berlin, barring the elected mayor from his office. The city's police force had been split into two. Berlin was a divided city. In the US, French and British zones the Western way of life continued, with its new German currency, its free newspapers and radio, and its free elections.

It now seems probable that neither the Western powers nor the USSR expected the clash over Berlin to become so prolonged, so desperate, or so dangerous. Each side, after the first week or so, gradually stiffened its own resistance and determination, and so was led into the most serious crisis of the early post-war years. But neither was willing to provoke all-out war.

After the Berlin Blockade: the Cold War Begins in Earnest

When the blockade ended, the USSR kept what it had had before: control of the eastern zone of Germany and the eastern sector of Berlin. The West retained its influence in the other zones, and in West Berlin. But both in East and West attitudes had hardened. The USSR said the West had

50

acted recklessly and needlessly. Most people in the West thought the USSR had gambled on taking control in West Berlin, and had lost. For the Germans themselves, the blockade strengthened their dislike of the USSR and improved relations with the Western powers.

The division of Germany became yet more distinct as a result of the blockade. Any peace treaty with Germany as a whole was now impossible.

The North Atlantic Treaty Organisation: The West Bands Together

The west Europeans were thoroughly frightened by the events of 1948. First Czechoslovakia had been brought under the control of the communists there, and that meant the end of its political freedom. Then the USSR had attempted to eject the Western Allies from Berlin, closing all access to the city. They responded by creating, with the USA, a powerful defence alliance: NATO, the North Atlantic Treaty Organisation.

The Earlier Treaties Which Led to NATO

1 March 1947: the British and French had formed an alliance by the Treaty of Dunkirk. The two countries would act together if either should ever again be attacked by Germany.

2 March 1948: The 'Benelux' countries (Belgium, the Netherlands and Luxembourg) were allied to Britain and France by the Treaty of Brussels. But by this time it was plain that European peace was unlikely to be threatened by Germany: it was Soviet plans these nations feared.

The trouble about these arrangements was that even when joined together these countries had nothing like the power which they would need to resist the USSR. That power could be provided only by the United States. Ernest Bevin, the British Foreign Minister, proposed that the alliance be expanded: to include the nations on the other side of the Atlantic — the USA and Canada. The result was the creation of NATO.

A Shield Against Aggression

The Times reported the signing of the North Atlantic Treaty on 4 April 1949 in Washington:

'The North Atlantic Treaty was signed this afternoon by the Foreign Ministers of the seven countries which originally negotiated the pact and the five others which were invited to join later... The ceremony was seen by hundreds of thousands on television and listened to on the wireless by millions more...

"In this pact", said President Truman, "it is hoped to create a shield against aggression and the fear of aggression ...". Mr Bevin, for Britain, pointed out that with the signing of the treaty "at last democracy is no longer a series of isolated units." Other Ministers added their own comments, the Italian saying that such a treaty could have prevented the two World Wars of 1914 and 1939. A note of caution was sounded by Canada's Lester Pearson. Signing the treaty held great promise of security, but only if the member states could "convert promise into performance", giving NATO the military strength it needed.'

Churchill at Boston: the Fourteen Men in the Kremlin

Whilst the treaty was being signed, Winston Churchill was also in the USA, as a private individual. He made a speech before a large audience at Boston. Why, he asked, had the Soviet government deliberately acted 'so as to unite the free world against them?' He gave his own answer, and it was one which many others in the West would also have given:

'It is because they fear the friendship of the west more than its hostility. They cannot afford to allow free and friendly intercourse to grow up between the vast area they control and the civilisation of the west... Fourteen men in the Kremlin, holding down hundreds of millions of people and aiming at the rule of the world, feel that at all costs they must keep up the barriers.'

The communist leaders in the USSR, said Churchill, had their missionaries in every country, waiting for the right time to take power; they had their anti-God religion; and 'behind all this stands the largest army in the world, in the hands of a government pursuing imperialist expansion as no Czar or Kaiser has ever done...

I must not conceal from you the truth as I see it. It is certain that Europe would have been Communized and London under bombardment some time ago but for the deterrent of the atomic bomb in the hands of the United States.'

NATO: a Defensive Alliance and a Counter-Attraction to Communism

The NATO alliance was defensive: the NATO forces could not go into action unless one of the members was attacked. But, in that case, an attack on one would be an attack on all. NATO also had a strong social and economic side. It would help all its members to develop their own cultures, and would extend trade between them. The treaty began by saying that member countries would guard the civilisation of their peoples, founded on democracy and individual liberty. NATO, said the Canadian Prime Minister, 'would not be merely negative. It would create the dynamic counter-attraction to Communism.'

The USSR and NATO

The USSR attacked the idea of NATO from the beginning. They said it was an offensive alliance aimed at them. They warned the smaller members that it would be a tool of America and Britain. They said it was contrary to the United Nations charter.

NATO members denied these claims. They pointed out that the USSR was itself already closely joined in military alliances with all the countries of eastern Europe. Together, these communist-controlled states already formed a powerful military bloc, linked by over twenty separate treaties. The UN charter permitted regional, defensive alliances. One American official declared that the USSR could easily prevent NATO's defence arrangements from coming into operation by 'the simple expedient of not attacking anyone'.

Soviet opposition to NATO became yet more bitter when, in 1951, Greece and Turkey became members. Turkey was a

'The Way it Happened – Ceremonial Signing of the Atlantic Pact.' A Soviet view of the NATO alliance, in which the West European nations which joined the alliance are seen as puppets of the USA

traditional enemy of the USSR, and to some Russians it seemed that with Turkey a member of NATO, the USSR was in danger of being 'encircled' in Europe. Later, in 1954, West Germany was also admitted to NATO. The reaction to this was remarkably strong, showing that Soviet fears of German strength were still very much alive.

The Communist Triumph in China

China's Great Day: Proclaiming the People's Republic

The clothes he wore were still those of a peasant. The crumpled cloth cap was the same too. Yet the man wearing them was not standing in his solitary cave but on top of a famous and colossal building overlooking a vast square filled with a multitude of tiny upturned faces — the people.

They were singing songs about him, they were shouting with a rhythmical roar, wishing him to live for 10,000 years.

He himself was barely visible to the multitude. But on the historic wall, right under the place where he stood on the terrace, hung a gigantic picture of his smiling face.

That picture, that cloth-capped head, that simple happy smile was seen during this year of victory in hundreds of cities. On tanks and on the boilers of railway engines, spread over the walls of tall buildings, on tiny flags in the hands of millions of children... everywhere the happy smile...

The date was 1 October, 1949. The place was Peking – the Gate of Heavenly Peace – from the top of which Chairman Mao Tse-tung issued a message to the entire world, solemnly proclaiming the establishment of the People's Republic of China.

Ten days previously Mao Tse-tung said

'We have united ourselves and defeated both our foreign and domestic oppressors by means of the People's War of Liberation and the People's great revolution... Our nation will from now on enter the large family of peace-loving and freedom-loving nations of the world... Our nation will never again be an insulted nation. We have stood up.'

When Mao and other Chinese leaders spoke of joining the peace-loving and freedom-loving nations of the world, they meant the communist bloc, at that time dominated by the USSR. They were eager to get on with the work of developing their new China, and they believed that their success earned them a place among the leading communist parties of the world.

Changing the New China

The Chinese communists had gained power in 1949 only at the end of a long and bitter civil war. Their enemies, the Nationalists, had received a good deal of support from the Americans — medical supplies, food, trucks, aircraft and vital munitions. Mao and his colleagues saw the United States as a hostile country.

Mao's government in 1949 included some non-communists, but it was plain to all that the Chinese Communist Party held firm, permanent control. Their success meant that from 1949 onwards the population of the 'Socialist Camp' was much greater than that of the NATO countries.

Communism in China was a very different thing from communism in Europe. It laid much greater stress on the importance of agriculture, and of the peasants. There was much to be done. Landlords were to be deprived of their estates, which were parcelled out among peasants. The vital irrigation systems of China — many thousands of kilometres of them — had to be repaired after wartime damage and neglect. Poor farmers had to be weaned away from old methods and taught better and more fruitful ways. Local warlords and groups of bandits which had plagued China for years had to be suppressed. Education and health care had to be brought to the vast countryside with its remote villages.

The New China and the West

It was China's foreign policies which concerned the West most urgently. Mao Tse-tung condemned 'American imperialism' as strongly as Stalin, or more so. He was furious that the United States continued to support his enemies, the Nationalists, who after 1949 were confined to the island of Taiwan. The USA made it plain that it would not allow Mao's forces to cross the straits and invade Taiwan. The Americans used their veto in the United Nations to prevent the People's Republic from taking a seat there: China continued to be represented by the Nationalists. The hostility between the new China and the USA grew bitter. The Americans refused to recognise Mao's government, and for years treated the defeated Nationalists on Taiwan as the true rulers of China.

Most people looked at the world situation in simple 'black and white' terms. Communists rejoiced that the 'Socialist Camp' now included China, as well as the USSR. They ignored vital differences between China and the USSR, and even between their communist parties. And to the West it looked as though the world was rapidly falling to communism, and that true democracy was in urgent danger.

Charting America's Foreign Policy

Truman Orders a Review

In January 1950 President Truman asked his experts to do a careful study on the US's future foreign policy. The background of world events against which they carried out this study seemed full of threats against the West. Within the previous two years:

1 Czechoslovakia had been ruthlessly taken under control by a minority of communists, acting with Soviet backing (February 1948);
2 Berlin had been blockaded by the USSR. Only the massive airlift had prevented the western zones of the city from falling under Soviet control (April 1948–May 1949);
3 The USSR had successfully produced an atom bomb (July 1949);
4 The long civil war in China had ended in communist victory. A Chinese People's Republic had been set up. (October 1949). An enormous bloc of communist states thus stretched from the Pacific Ocean to central Europe.
5 Communist guerilla armies were fighting for control of Indo-China and the Philippines.
6 The USSR and the east European states had formed a 'Council for Mutual Economic Assistance' (COMECON) in January 1949. This seemed likely to weld these communist states into a single industrial and trading unit.

President Truman's experts, in their discussions, foresaw 'an indefinite period of tension and danger' for America and the West.

A Blueprint for the Future: NSC 68

When it was produced, the study became known as NSC 68 (NSC = National Security Council). It was highly confidential, but its main lines have gradually become known to scholars. It mentioned four courses open to the United States. First, was the possibility of doing nothing, but simply continuing existing policies. Second, was the possibility of waging a 'preventive war' to stop any further Soviet expansion. The third course was to withdraw behind the shield of a 'Fortress America' and leave the USSR to do whatever it wished elsewhere in the world. These three courses were dismissed. The fourth possibility was the one recommended. This was 'a bold and massive program of rebuilding the West's defences to surpass that of the Soviet world'. The US, it said, 'should meet each fresh challenge promptly'. In time, it was hoped, the Soviet attitudes would soften, and world tension could then be eased.

Truman's Choice: America Must Lead the Free World

Truman accepted this last option: massive rearmament and powerful support for American allies. NSC 68 remained a secret document, but the chosen policy had somehow to be 'sold' to the American public. It meant great increases in defence spending, for American armaments and forces had been run down since 1945. It meant putting Kennan's idea of 'containment' into action round the world (see p. 20). It thrust the United States into the almost impossible task of policing the world against communism. It was to be the basis of US policy for the next twenty years. Above all, it meant that the USA was to become permanently, powerfully armed — quite unlike the America of pre-1941 days.

The USA did not enter on such a policy lightly. What finally persuaded many who were doubtful was the news which arrived from the far side of the Pacific on 25 June 1950. The armies of the People's Republic of Korea, Soviet-trained and equipped, had invaded south Korea. Communism, it seemed, was indeed out to dominate the world.

War in Korea

A Divided Country

Like Germany, Korea was divided between allied forces at the end of the Second World War. North Korea was occupied by Soviet forces, and South Korea by American. The 38° line of latitude separated these armies.

After a good deal of disagreement, and much discussion in the United Nations Organisation, American and Soviet troops withdrew from Korea, the last ones departing in the summer of 1949. But they left behind them a country still completely split: North Korea was a communist state, while South Korea, supported by the USA, was closer to the western style of democracy, though its government was a byword for corruption. Each of these governments claimed to rule all Korea. As in the case of Germany, everyone wanted the country to be reunited. But the rulers of the North, and the Russians, wanted a united, communist Korea. The Americans, and the South, wanted a republic patterned on South Korea. In 1949 and 1950 there were a number of clashes between soldiers of the two states along the 38th parallel.

The Attack on South Korea

On 25 June 1950 the forces of North Korea, equipped with Soviet arms, attacked the South. They quickly took Seoul, the southern capital, and pushed on to the south of the country. But the United States acted instantly. President Truman ordered troops to Korea; and on 27 June the Security Council of the United Nations asked all UN members to assist the South. It was only able to do this because the Russians had earlier in the year walked out of the Security Council and could not therefore use their veto. They were protesting at the exclusion of communist China from the UN.

The chance of a quick victory for the North disappeared.

Communist prisoners are marched into custody, guarded by American marines and tanks. Korea, September 1950

Instead, a bitter war developed which moved back and forth throughout both parts of Korea. Sixteen nations joined the United Nations command, including America, Britain, Australia and Turkey. The North also gained one powerful ally: China. Chinese troops crossed from Manchuria to assist them, and launched a vigorous assault on the UN forces in November 1950.

The war ended with a stalemate, an armistice being signed in July 1953. By that time the war had cost about four million casualties, of whom about one million were Korean civilians, caught up in fighting through no fault of their own. On the UN side, the brunt of the fighting, of the casualties and the expense, was borne by the USA. The USSR supplied weapons to the North, but took no part in the fighting.

Attlee Flies to Washington

Late in 1950, at a stage in the war when UN forces were retreating, the British Prime Minister Clement Attlee flew to Washington. The British parliament was alarmed that the Americans might spread the war to China. There was much talk in America of bombing the bases of the Chinese armies, and even of using the atomic bomb against them.

Attlee obtained Truman's agreement that Britain would be closely consulted. The bases were left alone, and atomic weapons were not used. But the incident showed that the USA and her allies might not always agree with one another. American leadership could not be questioned: but American policies and methods might be.

The Effects of the Korean War

Coming after the take-over of eastern Europe, and after the Berlin Blockade, the Korean War seemed to mean only one thing: communists, heavily backed by the USSR, were out to seize power — by force if needed — anywhere and everywhere the opportunity offered.

The USA was jerked out of any feeling of security it might have had. Congress voted huge sums to increase the US navy and army. 'Fight Communism!' became the popular slogan, and the greatest hero in America was General MacArthur, who had publicly said that the USA should use its power against mainland China. A similar sharp change of attitudes took place in Britain and in western Europe.

In Germany, the Korean War sharply affected public opinion. Many West Germans feared that they would be next on the communist list for attack. The Western powers were discussing the possibility of rearming West Germany; the Korean War made this a certainty. New German forces were in existence by the end of 1956.

The Cold War is Partly a War of Words

Distortions and Hysteria

The hostility between East and West was kept alive, not just because of policies and actions which the two sides carried out, but because of the barrage of words which came from leading politicians. Careless, sweeping statements were common. And it is clear that many politicians were in the habit of thinking about 'the other side' in ways which are too simple and misleading. When James Byrnes was US Secretary of State in the vital period 1945–7 he spent hours in fruitless argument with the Soviet Foreign Minister, Molotov. He commented that

'The people of whom Mr Molotov disapproves are always described as "Fascists". All communists and communist sympathisers are "democratic forces". It is a simple classification.'

It was also, of course a distortion — one which long remained part of communist thinking.

The West prides itself — rightly — on the freedom which individuals have to speak their minds. But this also results in expressions of foolish or naive attitudes. Thus, in the early post-war days when America alone possessed the atomic bomb, an American diplomat wanted the USSR to be warned to withdraw behind its own borders 'and if they refused I would use the atomic bomb on them while we have it and before they get it'. And the US Navy Secretary, in a speech at Boston in August 1950, actually called for a 'preventive war' against the USSR. Though he was disowned by President Truman, his words were quoted in the USSR, and their effect is easy to imagine.

The Tide of Anti-Communism in the West

The wave of intense anti-communist feeling was greatest in the United States. In some quarters anyone who wished to discuss communism seriously, or who asked whether it might have some good features, was likely to be labelled 'un-American'. Anyone referring to Karl Marx or Lenin without thoroughly condemning them might be branded as a 'red', and therefore unpatriotic. Since Marx's views and theories were important to anyone interested in nineteenth- or twentieth-century history, or politics, or economics, the wave of hysteria affected many students, teachers and writers.

It was not only communists who were affected by the crusade against them in the USA. People of moderate socialist views might be equally, and in their case unjustly, condemned. Even the Labour government in Britain had to withstand a good deal of criticism for what was thought to be its 'softness' towards communists or those who sympathised with them. As early as 1947 a US Army Intelligence Officer had 'widened the net' to condemn any but those of the most conservative outlook:

'A liberal is only a hop, skip and jump from a communist. A communist starts as a liberal.'

Some Americans tried to introduce a censorship of all American literature, extending it to bookshops, libraries, schools and colleges. They wanted to have all communist works such as the writings of Marx and Lenin, or even novels written by communists, banned. To do this would have meant destroying some of the very freedoms for which the USA stood. General Eisenhower, the Republican candidate for the Presidency, sounded a note of warning in 1952:

'Don't join the book burners...Don't be afraid to go to your library and read every book, as long as any document does not offend our own ideas of decency. That should be the only censorship. How shall we defeat communism unless we know what it is and what it teaches?'

McCarthyism

A few US politicians used the revulsion against communism for their own political purposes. The chief of these was a lawyer, Joseph McCarthy. He represented Wisconsin in the US Senate.

On 9 February 1950 McCarthy made a speech at Wheeling in West Virginia. It included a sensational charge that the American State Department itself (responsible for all foreign affairs) had been infiltrated by communists. There were, he said, over two hundred 'card-carrying communists' in this vital department of the US government. McCarthy went on to make further allegations, none of which he ever succeeded in proving. The Tydings committee which investigated his claims said they were 'a fraud and a hoax'. McCarthy was not the least daunted — the Tydings committee was mostly composed of Democrats, whereas he was a Republican: he saw their findings as political opposition.

McCarthy redoubled his efforts, making and repeating new charges on radio and television. According to him the government departments, armed services, schools and colleges were all penetrated by spies, saboteurs, or 'reds'. America was at risk from the hidden friends of the USSR and world revolution.

In 1953 the Republicans gained control of Congress, and McCarthy became chairman of an important Senate sub-committee concerned with investigations. It was a position of great power, and McCarthy used it vigorously, playing on Americans' fears of 'the red menace'. The committee's hearings were broadcast; anyone suspected of communism or disloyalty — 'un-American activities' — might be summoned before it and closely questioned about his political views over many years. The careers of many public employees were threatened or actually ruined by this system, and the victim had no redress. The accusations or insinuations were privileged — neither McCarthy nor the committee could be taken to court for remarks made inside Congress.

McCarthy's supporters claimed he was alerting the nation to perils within. But in reality McCarthy had become a threat to the very ideas of justice and freedom. His crusade became a farce when he named figures like the Secretary of the Army, and at one point even General Marshall — a former Secretary of State and the author of the European Recovery Programme. He even accused previous American governments — those of Roosevelt and Truman — of 'twenty years of treason'.

In December 1954 the Senate finally condemned McCarthy for his insulting behaviour and his abusive remarks about fellow-Senators. His influence then disappeared almost as rapidly as it had arisen, four years earlier. Those years had been an ugly period, in which some Americans, for a time, appeared to have lost their good sense and balance. The Cold War atmosphere had made 'McCarthyism' possible; McCarthyism in turn helped to sour relations still further.

The Warsaw Pact: a 'Mirror-Image' of NATO

Despite Soviet warnings, West Germany became a member of NATO in 1954. She was also allowed to rearm (see pages 74–5), though her forces were strictly controlled and limited, and she promised they would not be used to reunite Germany by force.

The USSR responded by creating the Warsaw Pact. It included all the communist states of eastern Europe except Yugoslavia. The armed forces of these countries were to be placed under one supreme commander, a Russian. Soviet troops continued to be stationed in four countries: East Germany, Poland, Hungary and Romania.

The Warsaw Pact was in some ways a 'mirror-image' of NATO, but in the communist world. It replaced the earlier military alliances by a single, central organisation, with its headquarters in Moscow. Its creation in 1955 put the finishing touches to the opposed military blocs: East versus West, communist versus capitalist. But there were two vital differences between the two blocs. NATO was composed of completely independent countries. They had chosen to come together, and could leave NATO if they wished. Long before the Pact was signed its member countries were firmly linked through their communist parties and through Soviet control. And on paper, the forces of the Pact were very much stronger than those of NATO, if nuclear weapons were discounted.

5 The Cold War after Stalin and Truman

New Leaders in East and West

In 1953 there were changes in the leadership both of the USA and the USSR.

In the USA: General Dwight Eisenhower became President. To take charge of foreign affairs he appointed as Secretary of State John Foster Dulles.

In the USSR: Stalin, the dictator, died in March. For a time, power lay in the hands of a small group of senior communists. Of these, Nikita Khrushchev was to emerge as the most powerful.

Dulles and Brinkmanship

Dulles was a strong anti-communist, believing that the threat of America's nuclear weapons would deter the USSR from aggression. It was necessary to treat the Russians with the utmost firmness, he believed:

'In crises that develop with the Soviet Union, the United States has to be prepared to go to the verge of war, if necessary. This is the kind of firmness and determination the Soviet rulers understand. By showing we are ready to go to the edge of war, we actually have a better chance of avoiding war...'

This attitude became known as brinkmanship. Dulles did not like this term, but he later claimed that this tough policy had prevented communist interference or gains in the Far East, in the Middle East, and in Korea. In the Far East China had been deterred from invading Taiwan; in the Middle East American marines were sent to Lebanon, at its request, to avert a civil war (1958); and in Korea the US threat to carry war into China by bombing produced, he said, the armistice of 1953.

Dulles spoke about 'rolling back' the USSR in Europe. He thought that firm policies would eventually force them to give up their control of the east European states. To the USSR, this looked like a policy of aggression and 'nuclear blackmail'.

Nuclear Confrontation

To base American policy on nuclear weapons seemed reasonable when only the USA possessed atomic bombs. But the USSR had produced its own atomic bomb in 1949. The USA had then gone ahead and, in 1952, had successfully tested the first hydrogen bomb. Hydrogen weapons were of much greater explosive power even than the first atomic bombs. Less than ten months after the Americans, the USSR too exploded a hydrogen bomb, in August 1953. The 'gap' seemed to be narrowing. Dulles's idea that any Soviet attack on the West could be met with 'massive retaliation'—meaning the use of nuclear weapons—began to look less and less reasonable in a world where both sides possessed such weapons.

The Legacy of Stalin

Nikita Khrushchev was the most powerful of the Soviet leaders from about 1955; his position was undisputed from 1958. He and other leading communists faced an agonising decision: what were they to do about the political prisoners 'left over' from the Stalin period? And what were they to say about the hundreds of thousands of murders carried out on his orders? It was decided to make a break with Stalin, denouncing his crimes. But this would be a very tricky operation indeed: the Soviet people had been taught to regard Stalin as all-wise, and a hero above all others. And foreign communist parties had to be considered—how would they react to the news that communism's hero had misused his power like any other dictator—say a Hitler or a Mussolini?

The Twentieth Party Congress, 1956

It was decided that Khrushchev should make the vital

'debunking' speech at the Twentieth Party Congress, in February 1956. 1400 delegates were present at the congress. They came to Moscow from all over the USSR, and there were also some who represented foreign communist parties. It was plain from the beginning that things had changed, for Stalin was criticised and some of his victims were openly praised. But nothing could have prepared the gathering for Khrushchev's speech—a mammoth performance of over 20,000 words. The atmosphere was electric, as Khrushchev himself tells us:

'The delegates listened in absolute silence. It was so quiet in the large hall you could hear a fly buzzing. You must try to imagine how shocked people were by the revelations of the atrocities to which party members—old Bolsheviks and up-and-coming young men alike—had been subjected. This was the first that most of them had heard of the tragedy which our party had undergone—a tragedy stemming from the sickness in Stalin's character.'

Stalin was condemned for his dictatorial rule over many years, for his persecutions, and for the many thousands of political murders he had ordered. Khrushchev provided example after example of the dictator's brutality, lack of humanity, or just foolishness. Stalin, he said, had perverted the purity of the revolution; on top of all this he had 'falsified history' to glorify himself. The debunking was very thorough: Soviet life could never be quite the same again.

The Effects of De-Stalinisation

Though Khrushchev's speech was given in secret session, copies were distributed to be read to party branches everywhere.

The effects were shattering. There was a ferment of discussion throughout the communist world. Statues of Stalin—hundreds of them—were destroyed in cities everywhere. Stalingrad was quickly found a new name—Volgograd. There was, for a time, a new freedom of discussion. But some 'hard-liners' resisted the change, finding it too much to alter existing habits of thought. Students at Tiflis university, in

Stalin's home region, rose in brief, violent protest as their local hero was suddenly cut down to size.

Khrushchev's speech had hardly touched on the USSR's foreign policy. But it deeply affected it nevertheless. The communist rulers in eastern Europe, except Tito, were all 'Stalin's men' — owing everything to him. In the angry discussions of 1956 they quickly came under attack. There were riots in Poland, and an actual revolt in Hungary (see p. 79). The Albanian communists flatly refused to dethrone Stalin. A split developed between them and Moscow. And, above all, there was increasing tension between the Chinese communists and the Russians. Four years later this was to become an open rift.

After 1956 it was no longer possible to view the communist-controlled states as a single group with only one foreign policy. The bloc was beginning to show cracks. Khrushchev acknowledged that there were 'different roads to Socialism'. He had somehow to steer his way through the difficult problems of the Cold War with all this at the back of his mind.

Khrushchev and Peaceful Coexistence

'War with the West is not Inevitable'

Khrushchev, though he had once been one of Stalin's henchmen, was a flexible, lively character. His memoirs — later smuggled out of the USSR — show that he was undoubtedly a sincere communist. He expected the end of capitalism. But he began in the fifties to gain the sort of knowledge which so many other Russians lacked. His visits to conferences abroad, and trips to America, Britain, France, India, Burma and elsewhere, gave him a growing appreciation of the rest of the world. And, although his manner was often rough and his tongue sharp, he tolerated criticism, and learned from it. He put no opponent, after 1953, to death. In these things he was a very great change from Stalin. He also knew that nuclear weapons made war between the two super-powers unthinkable. He began to stress the idea of 'peaceful coexistence', the notion that the socialist and capitalist systems could exist

68

side by side. Lenin had taught that a period of such coexistence was possible before the final conflict. Khrushchev altered the communist creed. He said that war with the West was not inevitable. Capitalism would collapse of its own accord. In 1958 he claimed in an interview with a British journalist:

'We do not have to teach the British, for example, to affect a revolution and establish the socialist system in their country. They will do it themselves when they come to realise that the system we have here, in the Soviet Union and in other socialist countries, presents greater advantages to the peoples than the capitalist system... Yes, we are convinced that our ideas will triumph. But victory for these ideas will not be won by war but by a higher standard of living under socialism.'

The stress on peaceful coexistence did help to produce some good results, and lessened some of the Cold War tension. Some of its results were:

The signing of a peace treaty with Austria in 1954;
The return by the USSR to Finnish control of the Porkkala naval base near Helsinki, in 1956;
The easing of travel restrictions in eastern Europe;
The abolition of the Cominform, which had attempted to get various national communist parties to work together, in 1957;
Khrushchev's visit to the USA in 1959. He was convinced by it that President Eisenhower wanted peace, and said as much; this infuriated the Chinese;
The signing of a Test Ban Treaty in 1963. By it the USSR, the USA and Britain stopped all nuclear tests except underground ones.

Catching up with America

Communists claimed continually that their way of organising society was far superior to that of the West. It would inevitably produce better results. This faith in communist planning led Khrushchev to say that the USSR would catch up the United States in its production and standard of living.

He rashly predicted in 1961 that this would happen in ten years. This proved hopelessly optimistic.

The Russians joked endlessly about this idea of catching up with America. Often, the jokes were in the form of questions which were supposed to have been put to a mythical radio station — the Armenian Radio:

Q   Why are Soviet citizens barefooted?
A   So they can run faster and consequently catch up more quickly to America.

Q   Will we catch up and surpass the Americans?
A   Yes, we will catch up to them, but we will not surpass them because then they would see the patches on the seats of our trousers.

Q   Where is the USA heading?
A   To catastrophe.
Q   Where are we heading?
A   We are trying to overtake and surpass them.

Perhaps such jokes will remind us that the Soviet people have always been noted for a sharp sense of humour. They may be less affected by their government's propaganda than we often suppose.

The Limitations of Peaceful Coexistence

Peaceful coexistence did not mean that the USSR gave up its aims — far from it. It would, said Khrushchev, compete with the West on every level; and would eventually triumph. It continued to promote communism throughout the world, supporting movements which it classed as 'progressive' even though most were struggling to overthrow existing governments. And Khrushchev made one thing abundantly clear: peaceful coexistence applied only internationally. There would be no tolerance for western, or anti-communist ideas *inside* the USSR. To allow a domestic opposition to communism was as unthinkable as ever.

Khrushchev continued to lash out hard at capitalism. In 1958 he explained the existence of the enormous Soviet army like this:

Police dogs guard the Fronau launching station near Berchtesgaden, in South Germany. The station sent pamphlets into Hungary, Czechoslovakia and elsewhere in the East. February 1956

'Since the ruling circles of the Western Powers, blinded by hatred for our country and the other socialist countries and for our communist ideas, wish to destroy us, we are compelled to maintain armed forces to protect the gains of our people.'

There were times when peaceful coexistence seemed to have failed utterly. There were crises over Hungary and Suez in 1956, over Berlin in the years 1958–61, and over Cuba in 1962. They posed the greatest threat to world peace — especially Cuba. Nevertheless, once these 'flashpoints' were passed, tensions were reduced.

The new stress on coexistence with the West is important for another reason. It cost the USSR the friendship and support of Mao's China. The Chinese communist leaders, at this period, still claimed war to be inevitable, and were furious at what they saw as Khrushchev's 'soft' attitudes to the West.

The Propaganda War Continues

East and West continued to bombard one another with propaganda, mostly by radio. Moscow put out the communist line; London and Paris provided an alternative news service in the east European languages. The Americans used their powerful transmitter in West Berlin for their 'Voice of America' broadcasts, beaming them to the peoples behind the Iron Curtain. For many years the broadcasts were 'jammed' by Soviet transmitters. There was also an American attempt, much resented by the USSR, to penetrate the East with pamphlets. These were conveyed by balloon, and released after a given time by the melting of dry ice, or by the bursting of a rubber container. It was an erratic business: some even ended up in Britain!

The Russians had a distinct advantage in this war of words and ideas. Their literature was obtainable, with very little trouble, throughout the West. But the Eastern bloc was closed to all Western news and comment, because of the universal censorship systems. Newspapers, novels, school textbooks — all had to conform to the Party's views.

6 Crisis Points

Germany

Adenauer Leads West Germany, 1949–1963

Konrad Adenauer became Chancellor of the German Federal Republic in 1949. The Republic was a new state, a democracy of the Western type. It had been created out of the former occupation zones of the three Western Allies. Adenauer's party, the Christian Democrats, won elections in 1953, 1957 and 1961. During this period the Republic became the most prosperous state in western Europe.

Adenauer was a Catholic who strongly opposed communism. His policies were staunchly pro-Western. He brought West Germany into NATO in 1954, and into the Common Market in 1957. He hoped to see Germany reunited some day, and refused to recognise the communist East German state which the USSR set up in its zone. He regarded the East German system as a denial of freedom.

Relations between the two Germanies became very bad indeed. They were members of rival alliances. There was a constant flow of refugees from east to west which weakened the eastern economy. East German leaders referred to Adenauer as a warmonger, bent on attacking the east. An East German document could describe West Germany like this in 1962:

'In the West German Federal Republic there prevail once again contempt for human beings, exploitation, . . . greed for money and conquest, and militarism. In other words, in the West German Federal Republic . . . there is kept alive everything in German history that is backward, barbaric and inhuman, stupid and cramped.'

Equally foolishly, some hot-headed West Germans spoke of uniting the country by force, and also of 'recovering the lost eastern provinces'. By this they meant the lands which the Poles had occupied in 1945 — Pomerania and Silesia.

West Germany became extremely prosperous in the 1950s, making a complete recovery from its 1945 devastation. The contrast between its wealth and the very slow progress of East Germany was stark and obvious. It seemed to put the difference between 'Western democracy' and 'communist democracy' on show for all to see.

1953: Riots in East Berlin and East Germany

On 16 June 1953 hundreds of building workers walked off a large housing project in East Berlin. The communist government had raised their 'work-norms' — the amount they were expected to do for a certain wage. The strike spread; there were noisy demonstrations against both East Berlin communists and the Russians. A news-stand selling communist papers and pamphlets was burned. Some of the People's Police were ill-treated; the red flag was torn down from the Brandenburg Gate where it had flown since 1945. The strikes and riots spread from Berlin to factories and mines throughout East Germany.

On the second day of the riots in Berlin the movement was so ugly that the People's Police could not cope with it. The Soviet commander of the city ordered his troops in. The tanks were confronted by youths throwing stones, and by crowds shouting 'Russians go home!' But they restored order. The demonstrations in various East German towns — Magdeburg, Goerlitz, Leuna, Stralsund and others — were dealt with in the same way. The communist hold on East Germany was as tight as ever. The riots were attributed by the communists to agitators who had crossed to East Berlin from the West to stir up trouble.

A New German Army: the Bundeswehr, 1956

Relations between East and West were very bad in the 1950s. This was partly due to the effects of the Korean War. There was fear in the West of a new war in which Europe

Soviet tanks clear the streets of East Berlin after the declaration of martial law, June 1953

might well be overrun by the large Soviet and east European armies. All attempts to get disarmament had failed. The governments of the USA and western Europe came to the view that a new West German army would have to be created to help restore the balance. This came into being in 1956: the *Bundeswehr*, or Federation Defence Force. It differed from all previous German forces, since it was firmly controlled by the West German Parliament, at Bonn. A small air force and navy were also created.

The USSR, and communists everywhere, objected fiercely to this new German force. They claimed it was intended for a new war against the USSR.

A Refugee from the East

Heinz Korner served throughout the war in the German army. When defeat came in 1945 he returned to his home in East Germany, and started an art firm. He published woodcuts, etchings, prints and lithographs. As the firm grew he found that he was subject to a sort of political censorship.

'Before reprinting or a new impression every sheet had to be submitted to Major Blechmann, the Soviet Cultural Officer. The major fixed his pince-nez and with his clever eyes gazed sceptically at the pictures as I fetched them from my portfolio. "Where are the Socialist work themes?" he would ask with his sharp shrill voice. "No workers' themes, no construction! That's bad!"

"Herr Major," I said, "these pictures serve the work of construction indirectly. When they look at these beautiful landscapes and themes like "Mother and child" the workers will be cheered and strengthened."

Such replies did not banish Major Blechmann's scepticism, but he passed most of my drawings and engravings.'

The currency reform of 1948 ruined Heinz's business, for he lost his customers in West Germany and West Berlin, and could buy no more prints from the West. His business was absorbed into a State Publishing firm, and he found himself commissioning portraits of East German politicians. 'The artists were paid well for their work; a litho of that kind cost ten marks in the shops of which the artist received three. Ministries, theatres, schools, factories, places of entertainment all had to buy these lithographs.' The East German public, however, were not so keen; 'we were left with 18,000 heads of Otto Nuschke—Nuschke was unsaleable'. Nuschke was a minor communist politician.

Heinz found himself under more and more restrictions:

'Nothing came over to us from the west, no publications about artistic controversies or developments, no art periodicals, nothing. I had the feeling that I was slowly starving. I kept travelling over to West Berlin to look at the exhibitions of modern art and longingly thumb the latest publications in the bookshops. Of course, it was discovered that I had 'western connections'. As a State employee, I was called on by our manager to give up my trips to West Berlin. That was an order. I fell into a deep depression. I could not live without contact with the west and western culture. So one day I went into the underground in the east sector with a portfolio under my arm—a small part of my collection—got out in West Berlin and have not returned.'

Heinz was one of more than four million citizens who fled from East Germany during the ten years ending in 1961. Some left because the state discouraged private business; many farmers because they were under great pressure to join collective farms. Others simply disliked the communist system, or wanted to share in the rising prosperity of West Germany. There was also a much smaller movement of people in the opposite direction.

A Capital City Divided: the Berlin Wall, 1961

The drain of citizens from east to west was a serious matter for the communist government of East Germany. The bulk of the refugees were young, trained and skilled: engineers, doctors, teachers and craftsmen who could ill be spared. The communists regarded West Berlin as a 'capitalist sore' in the midst of their socialist state, and a new German crisis arose in 1958–1961. The Soviet leader Khrushchev pressed hard for a German peace treaty — but on terms which would mean a communist triumph in both West Berlin and western Germany. The West refused these terms. It increased its armies in Germany, and sent an armoured group to Berlin.

In August 1961 the Soviets and East Germans acted. A barbed-wire barrier was erected to cut off the eastern sector from West Berlin. Then the wire was replaced by a wall of concrete blocks. Although there were a number of crossing-points left in the wall, these were reduced in the next few months, and were easily manned by police. Refugees could no longer flee easily from the east.

East Germany is Sealed off

After the building of the Berlin Wall, escape from East to West Germany became immensely difficult. Some managed it by tunnelling; some by swimming, where the border ran along Berlin's Teltow canal. Some managed to climb the wall, trusting that East German guards would deliberately take poor aim when ordered to fire at them. But many were unlucky, and were either caught, or injured, or killed in the attempt to cross.

West Berlin police protect the Berlin Wall with barbed wire, despite placards put up by protestors. August 1962

Peter Fechter Dies

Twelve months exactly after the barriers had first been erected across Berlin, on 13 August 1962, two young men tried to flee from the east across the wall. They were seen by guards as they ran across the open space on the eastern side. They ignored commands to halt. There was a flurry of shots. One of the two runners reached the wall and managed to climb over to safety. The other, an eighteen-year-old brick-layer called Peter Fechter, was hit. He fell right at the wall's base, wounded in the chest and stomach. His cries could be heard clearly, and West Berliners gathered to try to help. They tried to place a ladder over the wall, but were forced to stop by warning shots. They tried, in vain, to cut a hole through the rough concrete from the western side. All the while Fechter was in agony.

After an hour, four of the East German Police came and carried Peter away, to a chorus of hostile shouts from the west. In the evening the east Berlin press announced that 'a bandit' intercepted by police had died from his wounds.

78

The number of escape attempts became much less as East Germany too became prosperous in the 1960s. Living standards became the best in eastern Europe. With this prosperity the 'German problem' became slightly easier.

Hungary, 1956

An Old People under a Communist Government

The communists had gained complete power in Hungary in 1948. With Russian help, they set about making Hungary a socialist state. Many of the features of this new Hungary were an improvement on pre-1939 days. The enormous tracts of country previously controlled by a few aristocratic families, for example, were broken up and used for the good of the whole country. Though many of the peasants disliked the pressure put on them to set up collective farms, at least they had a more direct interest in working the land than in earlier times.

There were, however, many things in post-war Hungary which were bitterly resented. There was the complete control of education, which meant that children were taught Russian and communist history, and which ignored the fact that Hungary had for centuries been closely linked with western Europe, rather than with Asia. The deep religious faith of many Hungarians was frowned upon, and to ask for religious instruction for one's children was to put them at a disadvantage when it came to opportunities to enter college as teenagers. The Catholic schools had all been nationalised, and Cardinal Mindszenty, who had firmly opposed the communist influence on the church, had been tried for conspiracy and put in prison.

There was also dissatisfaction in industry. Workers felt they were toiling for very little reward, and knew perfectly well that many of the goods they produced were shipped off to the USSR, or went for export to Africa and elsewhere, with little benefit to Hungary. Then again, as in all the east European countries, the press, the theatre, all art and music were controlled. They had to 'serve the cause of socialism'.

Beyond all these grievances there were two features of

Hungarian life which aroused the greatest anger and resent-ment. The first was the AVO, or State Protection Group. This was an all-powerful secret police. It terrorised the people by the ruthless way it suppressed all criticism of the government, communism or the USSR. The second feature was the presence, eleven years after the war, of Soviet troops. Officially, they were there for Hungary's protection against the West. In reality they were a constant reminder that the country was dominated by her powerful north-eastern neigh-bour.

The Hungarians were an ancient, proud people. They were intensely patriotic. To make them good communists was not easy; to make them accept subordination to the USSR was a still greater problem.

The 'New Course'

After Stalin's death there was a 'new course' in government policies. Imre Nagy, the Prime Minister, led the way to a less strict sort of communism. Some peasants were allowed to leave the collective farms. More of the country's wealth went towards putting goods in the shops, instead of towards the constant building-up of heavy industry. The press was allowed more freedom, and some political prisoners were released. This new course was very popular.

Nagy's opponents — men who wanted the firmest com-munist control — hit back at Nagy in 1955. He lost power, and Hungary prepared for a return to firmer control. But on 23 October 1956 a revolution broke out in Budapest, Hungary's beautiful capital.

The Battle for Budapest

Laszlo Rigo was twenty-two when Budapest suddenly ex-ploded into revolution. He was a sergeant in the Hungarian army, and lived in the Kilian barracks in Budapest. His nickname, because of his sun-tanned appearance, was 'chocolate drop' — Chokki. He was a good communist, but like many others was to find that his Hungarian patriotism and his hatred of the AVO were to come first in any crisis.

Chokki heard firing in the centre of the town during the

evening of 23 October, and watched AVO men shooting into a large crowd gathered before the radio station. Hurrying back to his barracks he was in time to see a civilian who was attempting to get into the barracks shoot a soldier through the head. Chokki killed the civilian with a grenade, and discovered that he was an AVO major. Chokki and a group of soldiers then beat off an attempt by the AVO to take over the building with its stocks of ammunition. They were then besieged by civilians begging for arms, and after some hesitation the soldiers, both officers and men, gave out rifles, machine guns and cartridges.

Chokki and the men at Kilian knew that they would face an attack by Russian troops in the morning. There was little or no discussion of what they were doing. Since the AVO were supported by the Soviets, to fight the AVO meant fighting Russians. All night they prepared their positions and made petrol bombs.

'At 4 am an armoured car approached the barracks. Chokki, with six men, watched from the roof.

At the last unbearable moment they lit their fuses, held the bombs for a moment, then pitched them into the black night air. In marvellous arcs of sputtering flame they dropped toward the armoured car. The first bomb hit the pavement of Ulloi Street and exploded like a giant night flower blooming suddenly from the asphalt. It must have blinded the Russian driver, for the car lurched toward the wall of the barracks, where it absorbed in quick succession three bombs which set the entire vehicle ablaze. It staggered past the barracks, then its petrol tank exploded. This was the first recorded Russian casualty.'

More armoured cars followed. Some were destroyed, like the first, but their guns began to do terrible damage to the barracks, and there were many Hungarian soldiers killed and injured. Tanks followed: T-34s, sleek and menacing. But this time the barracks had received some odd reinforcements: young people from all over the city. One group of these, young mechanics, salvaged the gun from one of the derelict Soviet vehicles. Others, ranging down in age to as little as twelve years, jammed the cellars to await the assault. The tanks were met with a multitude of petrol bombs. Youngsters rushed out to ram pieces of heavy piping into the cog-wheels where the tracks ran. One group, operating from both sides of the street, fixed up a long rope to which they attached a bundle of heavy grenades. When these exploded under the tracks of a T-34 it was suddenly halted, barring the way to others, and an easy target for the petrol bombs.

The battle went on, not just by the Kilian barracks but elsewhere throughout central Budapest. More tanks were destroyed, and one was surrendered by its crew. On 29 October Soviet forces withdrew from the city. They left behind hundreds of dead, and many shattered, burnt-out vehicles and buildings. Chokki and his friends, for a few brief days, thought they had won.

Soviet Revenge: the Revolt is Crushed

After the six days of fighting, the Hungarians looked forward to changes. They wished for greater independence, and for an end to the Soviet occupation. Meanwhile, the tough old Cardinal Mindszenty had been found and released. Imre Nagy had been recalled to be Prime Minister once more. The first steps were taken to set up a new, more open kind of government — though still communist. Nagy declared that Hungary would leave the Warsaw Pact, and would become a neutral country. He demanded that Soviet troops leave Hungary.

At 4am on Sunday 4 November the Soviets came back, with artillery, planes, rocket batteries and tanks — the immensely powerful T-54s. The fighting was furious, despite the overwhelming superiority of the Soviet weapons. After six days, with the city in ruins, the resistance was over. It was a wonder the Hungarians had lasted so long. At the very lowest estimate, about three thousand of them had died. Another 20,000 had been wounded. This included many teenagers who had fought, with only the lightest of weapons, against heavily-armed Soviet infantry and tanks.

Imre Nagy, Hungary's Prime Minister, had taken refuge in the neutral territory of the Yugoslav embassy; Cardinal Mindszenty in the American.

Last Message from Budapest

A teletype link to Vienna remained open during part of the last Soviet attacks. A Hungarian reporter typed out these last messages to the West:

'We have almost no weapons, only light machine guns, Russian-made long rifles and some carbines. We haven't any kind of heavy guns. The people are jumping at the tanks, throwing in hand grenades and closing the driver's windows.

...What is the United Nations doing? Give us a little encouragement.

I am running over to the window in the next room to shoot, but I will be back if there is anything new...

The building of barricades is going on. The Parliament and its vicinity are crowded with tanks... Planes are flying overhead, but can't be counted, there are so many. The tanks are coming in big lines.

Our building has already been fired on, but so far there are no casualties.

The roar of the tanks is so loud we can't hear each other's voices.

In our building we have youngsters of fifteen and men of forty. Don't worry about us. We are strong, even if we are only a small nation — When the fighting is over we will rebuild our unhappy, much oppressed country.'

The Fate of a Prime Minister and a Cardinal

Imre Nagy, the Prime Minister who had wanted change, was tricked out of the Yugoslav embassy on 22 November. He was kidnapped by Soviet forces, tried in secret, and executed. His place was taken by Janos Kadar, leading a strict government which would cooperate fully with the USSR, for the time being.

In the American embassy the fiery old Cardinal Mindszenty was safe. He remained there for fifteen years. Eventually he was allowed to leave Hungary.

The Legacy of the Hungarian Revolt

The revolt of 1956, and the bitter workers' strikes which

83

followed it, made East-West relations tense and bitter. About 200,000 refugees left Hungary with grim memories of communism and Russian influence. They included Chokki, the Hungarian sergeant who had fought to defend Kilian barracks. Although Hungary was to grow much more prosperous in the 1960s, and some of the refugees later returned, a clear lesson had to be learned from the events in Budapest: the Soviets would not allow any of their satellite countries to go their own way, even if that way were a form of communism. If these nations were to find any form of independence, it would not be through armed revolt against communist police, or against Soviet forces. The West was powerless to help them; but the members of the NATO alliance became even more determined that there should be no further advance of Soviet power in Europe.

Suez, 1956

The very day after the Soviet assault on Budapest, British paratroops had landed in the Port Said area of Egypt (5 November 1956).

Britain and France jointly invaded the Suez Canal area after the failure of months of negotiations with Colonel Nasser, the Egyptian leader. He had nationalised the Canal, which both Britain and France regarded as vital to their prosperity; much of their seaborne trade depended on it. When the long-standing troubles between Egypt and Israel resulted in an Israeli attack across the Sinai desert towards the Canal, both Britain and France had a predetermined part in the Israeli plan. Their intervention was agreed beforehand.

The British-French attack achieved control of part of the Canal area. Before the operation could be completed the great outcry in the United Nations and the criticism of their action in the USA forced the two nations to halt, to allow the United Nations to send in a peace-keeping force.

The Suez Crisis had come at the wrong time for the Hungarians, helping to distract some attention from the tragedy of Budapest. The Soviets accused the British and French of 'old fashioned imperialism', and Khrushchev threatened them with rocket attacks; he afterwards claimed credit for having forced the invaders to give way. The USSR gained prestige in the developing world with its boast of rebuffing the 'empire-builders' in the Middle East. Colonel Nasser also gained by the Suez fiasco: the Arab nations afterwards revered him as the leader who had stood up to the West. The British and French lost in every way — the Canal was blocked for months, and was eventually run by the Egyptians without their help. For a while, it was clear that NATO was badly split over the Suez invasion. Their allies disapproved of the British-French action. It took time to rebuild the former trust among Western powers.

Cuba, 1962

A Revolution in one of America's Neighbours

Cuba went through a revolution in 1958. From then on the island was controlled by the government of Dr Fidel Castro, who had led his guerilla fighters down from the mountains to seize power. Castro overturned completely the corrupt system of his predecessor, General Batista. He then carried out much needed land reforms, and ended the abominable exploitation of Cuba's poor peasantry.

Castro was not, at first, a communist. But by 1962 he had become one, declaring himself a good 'Marxist-Leninist' and seeking the friendship and support of the USSR. Some of his changes in Cuba ruined American companies. They were confiscated, without compensation. Trade between Cuba and the USA broke down. Castro's fire-eating speeches made matters worse; so did the wave of anti-Castro feeling which swept the American press. Americans were appalled that a communist state had been set up on their very doorstep: for Cuba lay only about 240 kilometres south of the beaches of Florida.

The Bay of Pigs

US relations with Cuba reached the lowest possible level in April 1961. A group of about 1500 Cubans tried to topple Castro's government by mounting an invasion from the

USA. They were trained, armed, transported and supplied by the US's Central Intelligence Agency. They also had the blessing of the young American President, John Kennedy. Kennedy was later to wonder how he could have been so foolish as to let the plan continue.

The Cuban brigade landed on the south side of Cuba at the Bay of Pigs. Castro's small air force quickly destroyed two of their supply ships and shot down half of the eight B-26 bombers which had been 'lent' to the invaders. In three days Castro's forces were utterly triumphant and the invasion was crushed.

The Bay of Pigs was a fiasco for the United States. And it left both Castro and his Soviet backers looking anxiously for any sign of a further invasion from the USA.

Kennedy Faces a Crisis

11.45 am, Tuesday, 16 October 1962. A group of about twenty men assemble in the Cabinet Room in Washington. They are the top politicians and experts who deal with American defence and foreign affairs. They have been summoned urgently away from all other tasks by the President, John F Kennedy.

Photographic experts also arrive. They are from the Central Intelligence Agency (CIA). For many hours they have been examining hundreds of pictures taken over Cuba by a U-2 plane. Just a few of those photos have a special meaning. They are the reason for this extraordinary meeting.

The photos are displayed and examined. The CIA men explain what the tiny marks, blobs and lines mean. Soviet rockets, capable of carrying atomic warheads, are being installed in Cuba. In a fortnight or so they will be ready, and within their range lie Washington, New York and the majority of America's big cities.

The Build-up to Confrontation with the USSR

The Soviet build-up had been detected weeks earlier. Mig fighter planes had arrived. SAM anti-aircraft missiles had come in. The USA regarded these as defensive. But intermediate range rockets: they were a different matter.

The freighter *Kasimov*, carrying crated rockets for Cuba, is photographed at low level by an American aircraft. October 1962

The Americans monitored Cuba closely. Further U-2 flights were ordered and miles of film were used. More missile bases were found. Soviet ships at sea, heading for Cuba, were seen to be carrying the large rockets as deck cargo. Clearly, the Soviet statement on 11 September that no missiles would be placed on Cuba had been a lie.

Kennedy Broadcasts his Decision

After an anxious six days Kennedy made a television broadcast which was seen throughout the USA. At the same time the text was being broadcast in thirty-eight languages throughout the world. He gave the facts. He quoted the assurances he had received from the Soviet government about their activities in Cuba, commenting each time 'That statement was false'. He said he had ordered a blockade of the island. He declared that if any nuclear missile were launched from Cuba against the USA or its allies, this would be regarded as a direct attack by the USSR, 'requiring a full...response upon the Soviet Union'. And in a passage addressed directly to the Soviet leader, he said

'I call upon Chairman Khrushchev to halt and eliminate this clandestine, reckless, provocative threat to world peace and

87

to stable relations between our two nations. I call upon him further to abandon this course of world domination.'

'On the Edge of a Precipice'

For six days the crisis mounted. The reaction of the Soviets was furious. Their ambassador to the United Nations claimed that the photo evidence was forged – a clumsy move which showed the Soviets in a bad light. When faced with a direct question whether the USSR was building rocket bases in Cuba he could only bluster, and finally refuse to answer. Meanwhile, at least eighteen Soviet vessels still headed for Cuba. They were joined by Soviet submarines. Khrushchev, in Moscow, warned that the submarines would attack anyone interfering with the Soviet vessels. But in reality, the USSR was now up against an opponent at least as determined as itself:

'The US deployed 180 ships into the Caribbean. The Strategic Air Command was dispersed to civilian landing fields around the country to lessen its vulnerability in case of attack. The B-52 bomber force was ordered into the air fully loaded with atomic weapons. As one came down to land, another immediately took its place in the air.'

Around the world the sense of crisis, of possible imminent disaster, was complete. Robert Kennedy, the President's brother who was also a member of the American government, felt that 'we were on the edge of a precipice with no way off'.

Crisis Hysteria

Sometimes, in the heat of crisis, people will make statements which would best be ignored. Thus, whilst the world was appalled at the prospect of war which was developing, a party was held at the USSR's embassy in Washington. It had long been arranged, and diplomats and officials tried to engage in small talk and forget the tense situation. But the pressures became too much for one Russian. 'I fought in three wars already and I am looking forward to fighting in the next' declared Lt. General Dubovik, mopping his brow. 'We

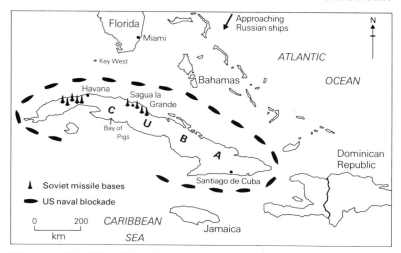

The scene of the Cuban Missile Crisis

Russians are ready to defend ourselves . . . our ships will sail through . . . ' Of course his words, the product of tension and worry, were widely reported. Everywhere, the stress of the crisis added its own weight to the problem facing Washington and Moscow.

'The Soviet Ships have Stopped'

On Wednesday, 24 October 1962, came the first signs that gave the world some hope of peace. Twenty of the Soviet ships had stopped. Some reversed course. There was an exchange of letters and telegrams. Then, on 26 October, Khrushchev offered to remove the rockets, in exchange for a promise that the US would not invade Cuba. American plans for such an invasion were within two or three days of being carried out.

The missiles went back to the USSR, with every movement being watched by American aircraft right back to the Soviet ports. The sites were ploughed over. The USA gave its guarantee that it would not invade Cuba.

The Lessons of Cuba

The Chinese were furious that the Russians had 'backed

down' over Cuba. Their words seem to indicate that they wanted a Soviet-American clash, despite the horror it promised.

Castro was also furious: the deal to withdraw the missiles had been made over his head. He refused to allow United Nations observers into Cuba to check that the sites were being dismantled. He turned away from the USSR for a time, developing his own brand of American communism.

"Let's Get A Lock For This Thing"

Kennedy, Khrushchev and the Cuba Crisis. It suddenly became brutally plain that East and West did have something in common after all – fear of nuclear war

Khrushchev later claimed that he had 'won' all he wanted: the American promise not to invade.

Kennedy was impressed by the frighteningly great need for care in dealing with such crises. He had seen how easy it would be to stumble into war through simple ignorance or miscalculation. He realised how important communications between the powers were. At times, when hours counted vitally, he and Khrushchev had had to rely on ordinary press channels to get their messages passed quickly between Moscow and Washington. Both he and Khrushchev decided that there needed to be much better methods of 'crisis management', so that neither side could misunderstand the other. A direct 'hot-line' was set up, linking the two governments by tele-type.

Czechoslovakia, 1968

The Prague Spring

In January 1968 the Czechoslovak communists elected a new leader—Alexander Dubcek. There had already been a slight loosening of the tight control the communist government exercised. Under Dubcek this thaw became a flood. There was a spate of discussion and debate over politics. New newspapers appeared, criticising previous communist leaders for their mistakes, and their suppression of the Czech people. In its 'Action Programme' Dubcek's government even went so far as to declare that the Party's role must be strictly limited: it could never be the 'universal caretaker' of Czechoslovakia. This was an amazing retreat, considering its firm control over all parts of Czech life. Even more surprising, the programme firmly stated that 'we must have an end to delayed, distorted and incomplete news.' In June 1968 the government censorship was abolished. It was an exciting time—a marvellous springtime in which a new patriotism and freedom swept over the country.

Dubcek was careful to make it clear that Czechoslovakia was still loyal to the 'socialist camp'. She remained within the Warsaw Pact. But the Russians were hard to convince. They held large army manoeuvres just outside the Czech borders. They were appalled by the new freedom of the Czech newspapers, and at proposals like that to allow freedom of travel to the West.

The Soviet Invasion

On 20 August 1968 Soviet tanks rolled into the country. Poland, East Germany, Hungary and Bulgaria also sent troops to take part in the invasion. Dubcek was taken in

Czech crowds in angry dispute with a Soviet tank crew, August 1968

handcuffs to Moscow. The Czechs were powerless to resist.
But they made their fury plain to the invaders. Under Soviet
influence a new government was created, which undid most
of Dubcek's reforms. The USSR had shown once more that
there was a severe limit to the amount of freedom which it
would allow the satellite countries.

The Brezhnev Doctrine

Brezhnev, the Soviet leader who had replaced Khrushchev,
called the invasion 'coming to the aid of a fraternal nation',
though it was quite plain that no one in Czechoslovakia,
communists or non-communists, had wanted the invasion.
He said that if hostile forces tried to turn any member away
from the 'socialist camp' in the direction of capitalism, it was
the duty of other members to intervene. This idea became
known as the 'Brezhnev Doctrine'. It was denounced by the
West, and also by the Chinese, by the Romanians, by Tito in
Yugoslavia, and by the Communist parties in western
Europe. It thus caused a bad split in communist ranks, and
led many to forsake communism altogether.

7 East-West Rivalry: The Intelligence Race

Spies of the Cold War: 2 Rudolf Abel

Defection in Paris

In May 1957 a man walked into the American embassy in Paris and confessed to spying for the Soviets in the USA. He was a Finn, and a rather shifty character with a great liking for vodka. He supported his story by producing one of the special gadgets given to him to help in passing on secret messages. It was a coin, cleverly machined into two parts so that a microdot message could be hidden inside. He explained that he had been ordered back to Moscow — was indeed on his way — but did not want to return. He provided information about his chief in the USA, whom he knew only as 'Mark'.

Tracking Down a Resident Spy-Master

Back in New York, the FBI set out to track down 'Mark'. Following the rather scanty information given, they kept watch on an artist's studio in Brooklyn. Eventually a middle-aged, balding man turned up late at night, stayed some time, and then left. He was tailed, but the trackers lost him somewhere in the city. It was three more weeks before they had another chance. After another late-night session in the studio he was followed to the Hotel Latham. The watch continued: then about 7.30 a.m. on 21 June the quarry was arrested.

It was one of the greatest feats the FBI had ever pulled off. Searches revealed dozens of damning items: tiny rolls of microfilm, concealed in a hollow pencil; radio receivers and transmitters; and many thousands of dollars. One of these items led the FBI to an army master-sergeant who admitted he had worked for the Russians. The man the FBI had arrested was Colonel Rudolf Abel, of the Soviet Secret Service, or KGB.

Abel was a very experienced Soviet agent. He had worked inside the German army during the war — and they had even decorated him. In the USA he was chief of operations, running a whole network of spies throughout North America. All the while he had kept up his 'cover' personality, as Emil Goldfuss, a Brooklyn painter. His trial, later in 1957, helped to convince Americans of the seriousness of the efforts the Soviets were making to discover their defence secrets. When we remember that it was also at this period the Russians showed their mastery of large rockets by launching the sputniks (p. 101), it is no wonder Americans came to think of themselves as engaged in a deadly race with the USSR.

Spies of the Cold War: 3 Gordon Lonsdale and the Portland Spy Ring

Letter from Behind the Iron Curtain

Late in 1959 the American Ambassador in Berne, Switzerland, received an important letter. Enclosed in it was a sealed envelope, and a request that it should be passed on to the secret service. It was given to the CIA (Central Intelligence Agency). It turned out to be the first of fourteen letters from someone who gave himself the code-name 'Sniper'. It offered the Americans information about Soviet spying activities in the West. 'Sniper' later defected and went to America. He was a Polish army intelligence officer.

Among the details given by Sniper was the fact that Royal Navy secrets were being betrayed by someone in a trusted position. This traitor, according to Sniper, had once been posted at the British Embassy in Warsaw. It was there that he was first approached by Soviet or Polish agents. The British checked through their files, and their suspicions narrowed to one man: a clerk at the naval base at Portland, in Dorset. His name was Harry Houghton.

Closing the Net on a Spy Ring

Houghton was closely watched. He was plainly 'living beyond his means' — that is, spending much more money than his job paid him. His friend Ethel Gee, also a worker at Portland, was seen to be closely involved: she was taking secret documents from a strongroom and passing them to Houghton to be photographed.

In June 1960 the watchers from MI5* found that Houghton was having regular meetings with a small businessman called Gordon Lonsdale. At these meetings, in London, documents would be handed over. Eventually the watchers saw Lonsdale deposit a briefcase and a stout steel box at the Midland Bank in Great Portland Street, London. A search warrant was obtained. Confronted with this, the bank manager allowed MI5 to examine the box and the briefcase. They contained a camera and film, a tabletop lighter with secret compartments built into it, a timetable which gave times when radio messages should be transmitted, and a magnifying glass. Hidden in the lighter was a device well-known to all spies: a 'one-time pad', used for sending messages in virtually unbreakable code.

Lonsdale was a difficult man to track. He constantly looked around to see whether he was being followed, and was obviously very alert. Despite this, the watchers observed him making many visits to a bungalow — 45, Cranley Drive, Ruislip. This was owned by a bookseller, Peter Kroger. He and his wife were obviously on very close terms with Lonsdale.

The Arrest

On Saturday, 7 January 1961, Houghton and Gee drove from Portland to Salisbury, where they caught the London train. Their progress was watched and reported at every stage by British agents. Ethel Gee carried a shopping bag. There were secret papers in it which gave details of HMS Dreadnought — Britain's first nuclear-powered submarine.

---

* Military Intelligence, section 5; responsible for counter-espionage and security matters.

Houghton and Gee arrived at Waterloo Station. They caught a bus and went to a street market, still tailed by a team of watchers. Detective Superintendent Smith, who was in charge of this part of the operation, received a report that Lonsdale had left his London flat and was heading to join them. A short time later Lonsdale parked his car and walked along by the Old Vic theatre. Houghton and Gee passed him on the pavement. A moment later Lonsdale turned, caught them up and greeted them. He took the shopping bag from Gee. Then, as the three walked along together, Superintendent Smith stepped in front of them, told them who he was, and said, 'You are all under arrest'.

A Radio Station in a Bungalow

Lonsdale, Houghton and Gee were taken to New Scotland Yard in separate cars. Superintendent Smith raced over to the bungalow in Ruislip. He asked the Krogers for details of the man who visited them, Lonsdale. Although the Krogers appeared helpful and mentioned numbers of people, they kept quiet about Lonsdale. They were taken to the Yard.

Number 45, Cranley Drive was searched. It yielded some amazing secrets. There were large sums of money concealed. There was a powerful, modern radio set and instructions about call signs and wavelengths. There were false passports and photographic equipment. There was a request, in poor English, for details of British anti-submarine devices. And there were many common objects which had been carefully altered to make secret hiding places. These included a torch battery, a tin of talcum powder, a hip flask and a pair of bookends. In Mrs Kroger's handbag were found three 'microdots' — tiny photographic negatives which when enlarged turned out to be letters in Russian.

There was much more evidence too. The bungalow was a spy centre. Radio experts listened in at the times given in the papers found concealed in the table lighters, and using the wavelengths indicated. Sure enough they picked up coded messages which direction-finding equipment showed came from near Moscow.

All five spies went to prison. Lonsdale was given twenty-five years, the Krogers twenty, and Houghton and Gee fifteen. Lonsdale was however exchanged for Greville Wynne in April 1964, and the Krogers were similarly exchanged in 1969.

Spies of the Cold War: 4 Greville Wynne

The British Businessman and the GRU Colonel

Greville Wynne was a British businessman who specialised in trade with eastern Europe and the USSR. He represented a number of electrical and engineering firms. On occasion he had also acted on behalf of the British intelligence services. In 1960, during discussions in Moscow with Soviet officials, he met a Russian who was to prove very important in the 'spy war' – Oleg Penkovsky.

Penkovsky was of very high rank in the GRU: the Military Intelligence Organisation of the Red Army. He had a distinguished war record, and he was married to the daughter of a top-ranking general. Though he had been a loyal communist for many years he had gradually come to see that there was a great gulf between the Soviet people, whom he loved, and the few hundred thousand politicians and officials of various kinds who ran the country. And in 1960 Penkovsky believed that the Soviet policies were reckless, misguided, and might well lead to nuclear war. He decided to 'come over' — giving the Western governments all the information possible about Soviet plans and intentions.

A Walk in Red Square, April 1961

Wynne had been discussing arrangments for a visit of Soviet engineers to Britain. Afterwards he walked with Penkovsky across Red Square. The two men were by this time on good terms, Penkovsky being known to Wynne as 'Alex'.

'Look, Alex. I'm none too happy about this list of names. ... You know these aren't the qualified people I asked for. They're minor officials...' 'Does it really matter all that much?' asked Alex. 'It certainly does. My companies are expecting experts. ... I'll have to bring it up before the committee.'

Suddenly Alex grasped the sleeve of Wynne's coat. 'You

must not do that. They would cancel the visit, cancel it
entirely... Greville... They've given me permission to go. It
is I who must go to London. Not for pleasure. I ... I have
things to bring with me ... Papers. Important papers. Your
government must have them.' He was very agitated.

The two men stopped and faced one another, in the
middle of the broad square. Alex hinted at the people whom
he knew would want his information: 'You know, important
people ... not politicians ... not the police.' Wynne decided
instantly to trust him and reveal his own connections with
the Secret Service. 'I know the people you mean', he said.
'They are my friends.' Penkovsky stood stock still, amazed,
for a moment. Wynne repeated 'They are friends of mine.'

Penkovsky took the plunge: 'Then you must take these
documents out with you. But I must have your promise ... I
want you to give them to a man you can rely on absolutely...'

Later that day Alex handed to Wynne a large envelope. In
it were secret minutes of important Russian committees, a
letter with Khrushchev's signature, and details of the USSR's
rocket sites. And just before Wynne left Moscow, on the
following morning, Alex gave him further confidential papers
which established, beyond any doubt, that the Soviet colonel
was prepared to assist British intelligence.

Debriefing in London and Paris

Penkovsky visited the West three times in 1961 — accom-
panying trade delegations to Paris and London. Regularly,
during the night, he met with intelligence men from Britain
and America at secret hideouts, passing on information and
answering hundreds of questions. He told of Red Army
battle plans, of the existence of secret factories where important military equipment was produced, and about the Soviet
plans for producing giant inter-continental rockets. He also
warned that the USSR intended to set up missiles in Cuba.
All this information was shared between Britain and America
for the two countries had agreed to work jointly over Penkovsky.

The Soviets became suspicious of Penkovsky sometime

during 1962. Wynne had made elaborate arrangements to smuggle Penkovsky out to the West if his position became dangerous. Two large exhibition caravans had been constructed to Wynne's own design, and there was a secret compartment in one of them where a man could be hidden. But it was all in vain. Penkovsky was arrested on or about 22 October, and Wynne himself was picked up a few days after in Budapest. They were both brought to trial, and Penkovsky was sentenced to death. Wynne got eight years; but after little more than a year he was released in exchange for Konon Molody, who had spied in Britain under the name Gordon Lonsdale.

'There Are Russian Spies' — Moscow

It was only a short time after the trials of Wynne and Penkovsky that the Russians admitted that there were such things as Soviet spies, working against the West. Until then they had always denied their existence. Spies, according to Moscow, were always in the pay of the Western powers, and were corrupt, or bestial, or decadent. In the mid-sixties this policy was changed and the stories of some Soviet agents were released in the form of films, television plays or books. In each case the spy was shown as a Soviet hero, working for the highest motives. Western observers noted that the stories had all been carefully censored, and in some cases, falsified.

The Scale of the Intelligence War

'Spy-trials' have taken place at intervals, both in the West and the East. They have built up a disturbing picture. Both sides in the Cold War run powerful, extensive, intelligence services. Spying is a more widespread activity than ever before.

The Central Intelligence Agency

We know most about the Western services. Though both Britain and France have their own systems, by far the most important is the American Central Intelligence Agency (CIA). Since 1947 the CIA has spent vast amounts of money on secret work. Its more spectacular successes included the digging of a 550 metre tunnel into East Berlin, to connect its own wires to a vital telephone exchange; and the organisation of the U-2 reconnaissance flights over the USSR. It has also acted to overturn governments in small states. When Guatemala had a pro-communist government from 1951 to 1954 the CIA helped to bring about its overthrow by supporting its chief opponent. The CIA's reputation was, however, . badly damaged by the failure of the 'Bay of Pigs' attempt to invade Cuba in 1961. It organised the invasion, but gave the President a woefully optimistic view of the project's chance of success. Its activities were closely scrutinised in the 1960s and it became more closely controlled by the government.

KGB and GRU

Our knowledge of Soviet spying comes mostly from a steady stream of defectors who have fled to the West. The main bodies concerned are the Committee for State Security (KGB) and the Military Intelligence Unit (GRU). These operate a world-wide network of spies and agents. They recruit everywhere, in rich and poor countries alike, and seek military, political and industrial secrets. Their recruits have often been communists, or communist sympathizers, but many have also been obtained by blackmail. Like the CIA, the KGB has tried to topple or discredit governments — those which annoyed the Soviets. These included both the Egyptian and Sudanese governments. KGB officers often work from Soviet embassies, holding 'cover' positions as chauffeurs, clerks, secretaries or attachés. The work of the KGB is not, however, confined to the world outside the USSR. Inside the USSR it plays a vital role, controlling Soviet society for the Communist Party. The KGB's work in the West is complemented by agents from the east European countries, particularly Bulgaria and Poland. These have been detected in seeking information, recruiting important army, navy or air force members, and committing political murder in Western cities, including London.

8 Confrontation and Competition, 1957–1962

Sputnik Circles the World and Goads the US into Action

The Missile Conference in Washington

4 October 1957. The international conference in Washington listens to papers from experts. Members spend the evening drinking and talking. Much of the discussion centres on rockets. Both the USA and the USSR are developing these. The scientists know that eventually the world may have to face the problem of the very large rocket—the Inter-Continental Ballistic Missile or ICBM—which will be able to attack distant countries across thousands of miles. When that day comes, the two Great Powers will no longer be safe and secure from attack inside their borders.

The conference is part of the special arrangements for the International Geophysical Year. Many countries have promised to undertake special projects for this.

The head of the Soviet group is Dr Blagonravov. Chatting with others, he gives no hint of the secret he carries in his head. His colleagues in the USSR will try to launch the world's first artificial satellite while the conference is in session.

Around the World in Ninety-five Minutes

Around midnight the story breaks. A Moscow broadcast announces that Russia has put a satellite into orbit. It is, in fact, racing around the earth at the unbelievable speed of 28,000 kph—about 8000 m every second! What is more, it is not the tiny, apple-sized object which those in the know might have expected. It is as big as the best pumpkin, and astonishingly heavy (58 cm in diameter and 84 kg in weight). The Soviets call it 'Sputnik', which means 'Traveller'.

Over the next days and weeks amateur astronomers and radio operators all over the world search eagerly for the Soviet spacecraft as it orbits, hundreds of kilometres above. On 6 October it is seen in the night sky over Tasmania, moving steadily onwards like a bright star. It is picked up in Canada, the USSR, Scotland and various parts of Europe over the following week. Even in cloudy weather it can still be tracked by its radio signals: a rapid 'bleep, bleep' endlessly repeated on the seven- and fifteen-metre bands.

The news is greeted with astonishment in America. The US has been used to thinking of itself as the world's leader in this sort of space and rocket work. Blagonravov is besieged by reporters wanting further details. He explains that the sputnik is 'the simplest kind of baby moon'. In a TV interview he says that no one has anything to fear from the Soviet sputnik — it is for research, to learn about space and space travel. Americans, and everyone else, however, cannot help noticing that in a matter of a week it has passed over all the world's great cities, many two or three times.

Laika: Space Husky

Another Soviet sputnik was thrust into earth orbit about a month later. This time it weighed about half a tonne (508 kg), and carried a variety of apparatus. It also carried a dog: a husky called Laika. Blagonravov told how the dog had been trained for its flight, and how it was provided with food and drink 'for more than just a few days'. Laika's breathing, heartbeat and blood pressure were all continually measured and radioed back to the USSR. However, when it became known that there were no arrangements to bring Laika back to earth there were swift protests from animal lovers.

The Meaning of the Sputniks for the Cold War

Sputniks were a fine scientific achievement — the forerunners of much excellent research both in the USSR and in the West. But for those concerned with defence they carried another meaning. To thrust sputniks of such weight into such high orbits demanded enormous rockets. Plainly, the Soviets had solved the problem of the ICBM: they had

The Moscow monument which commemorates the sputnik launchings of 1957

rockets which could if desired blast their way across the whole of Europe to reach France or Britain, or soar across the Arctic to hit the New World itself. Later versions of the sputniks could be used to photograph the lands beneath them.

There was uproar in the US. One senator said that the country was facing 'a new and terrifying danger'. Another described the sputniks as 'a devastating blow to the prestige of the USA'. One American working on the USA's own satellite programme spoke for millions when he said: 'Frankly, its enough to scare hell out of me. If they can do that, they can drop ICBMs on us.' Sputnik had set the alarm bells ringing in the US.

The Russians were naturally proud of their achievement. *Pravda* newspaper of 8 October 1957 put the communist view like this:

THE GREAT VICTORY IN THE PEACEFUL COMPETITION WITH CAPITALISM

'The launching of the artificial earth satellite is a victory for Soviet man, who with Bolshevik boldness and clearness of purpose, determination and energy, knows how to march forward. This is a victory for collective labour, the one and only system which is capable of creating real wonders in the world.'

The 'Space Race' gets into Top Gear

The Americans acted swiftly. Cuts in their space programme were instantly cancelled. Congress created new space committees, controlling the expenditure of billions of dollars. President Eisenhower appointed a 'Special Assistant for Science and Technology', who was to monitor progress on defence. Rocket work was given the highest priority, so that the first American satellite went into orbit on 31 January 1958. Within a year the US announced 'Project Mercury' which was to put men into orbit; and NASA, the National Aeronautics and Space Administration, was created and seven astronauts chosen. Ten years later, an American was to land on the moon.

There was one other by-product from the sputniks. The Americans took a close look at their whole educational system, which was failing to produce enough scientists. Over the following years science and technology received a tremendous boost in American schools, colleges and universities. Sputnik had created a new awareness of the Cold War in the United States.

An Interception Mission: A Soviet Bear off Scotland
Testing NATO's Flank

In the 1950s Soviet aircraft would often probe NATO's defences. They would fly close to some sensitive area, testing the speed of NATO reactions. They frequently used their

A Soviet 'Bear' aircraft, photographed from a NATO interceptor, whilst on long-range ocean patrol, 1968

large Tupolev aircraft, which the West code-named 'Bear' or 'Badger'. These aircraft had very long ranges, and were packed with sensitive equipment. They would record as much as possible about NATO radar and radio systems, and would obtain 'fixes' on the transmitters.

On a typical mission the Bear heads out from the USSR's Archangel region over the cold seas to the north of Norway. This is NATO's northern flank, and the Bear is picked up by long-range radar in Norway. As the Bear turns southwards and sets course for the Faroes Gap and the Scottish coast, RAF Strike Command is alerted. Word is passed to the RAF station at Leuchars, which has interceptor aircraft ready. The Bear becomes visible on British radar, and the gap narrows rapidly.

Interception

'At RAF Leuchars two Lightning aircraft, housed in a small, special hangar, are poised ready to go. Their fuel tanks are full, and the Red Top missiles clamped to their sides are live and deadly. Their pilots too are ready, even taking meals whilst wearing their heavy rubber suits.

A box on the wall squawks. The pilots dash quickly to their cockpits. Hangar doors are already open, and in a few seconds the Lightnings roar down the runway, afterburners blazing, and begin a swift climb to 10,000 m. The voice of their ground controller gives them a course.

Within minutes of crossing the Scottish coast the Lightning pilots see the Bear straight ahead. Its pencil-thin body bulges with domes, aerials and blisters. The latest Russian electronic equipment is at work, seeking to learn what it can of the NATO defence networks.

The Bear is over international waters: it has nothing to fear. But it now has an RAF escort, watching it closely, and photographing it too. It will be under close watch till it turns for home. As it does so, one of the crew, visible quite clearly behind one of the blisters, waves a gloved hand. NATO's response has again been tested.'

Both East and West use intelligence gathering aircraft like the Bear. Ships are also used, packed with the means for picking up and recording anything which can help to give a picture of the defences of 'the other side'. In the Far East, American intelligence vessels have occasionally been attacked and detained; and more than one survey aircraft has been shot down, though in neutral airspace.

Spies of the Cold War: 5 The U-2 Plane

In 1956 the American Central Intelligence Agency began to use a remarkable new plane. It was the U-2, designed and developed by the Lockheed Corporation to fly at enormous altitudes and to have a tremendous range — approaching 6400 kilometres. When equipped with cameras and sensitive radio receivers the U-2 was a superb aircraft for spying. A series of spy flights began over the USSR, with the U-2s gathering military information of great importance. For a time the Soviets were powerless to interfere with the flights.

U-2s photographed the latest Soviet nuclear bombers, known in the West as 'Badger' and 'Bison', on their airfields; they found the USSR's huge inter-continental rockets at their testing ground near the Aral Sea. They also began to fly over communist China in 1957. A stream of valuable military information was produced by the flights — about thirty in all.

Spy-Flight Over the Soviet Union

On 1 May 1960, Francis Powers took off in a U-2 from the

US base at Peshawar, Pakistan. He crossed into the USSR, the peaks of the Hindu Kush mountains far below him. His altitude was later said to have been 24,400 metres, but it may in fact have been even higher than this. At such immense heights—20 kilometres and more—no Soviet fighter could hope to reach him. He also thought that he was beyond the reach of any anti-aircraft weapons.

Powers flew steadily northwards over the USSR, intending to land in Norway, where there was another US base. At intervals he switched on the equipment he carried—five separate systems for gathering intelligence. Soviet military depots, missile bases, airfields and many other features were all photographed in staggering detail by the U-2's cameras. Its tape recorders picked up the radio signals and the radar impulses from the Soviet anti-aircraft defences far below.

The flight went well until Powers reached the Sverdlovsk region. There the U-2 was brought down, according to the Soviets, by an anti-aircraft missile. Powers was captured, and the films and tapes recovered from the wrecked plane.

The Paris Summit

In Paris, preparations were well advanced for a 'summit' conference between Soviet and Western leaders. The main subjects for discussion were the possibility of reuniting Germany, and of a German peace treaty. Both the USA and the USSR had built up immense stocks of missiles with which they could threaten one another's very existence, and there was hope that the conference might lessen the tension. Both de Gaulle and Macmillan, the French and British leaders, shared this hope.

On 7 May 1960 Khrushchev, for the USSR, announced that Powers would be put on trial in Moscow. Eisenhower, the American President, claimed that the USA had the right to gather intelligence in any possible way, since the USSR, unlike the USA, was a 'closed society'. The delegations arrived in Paris. The Russians made renewed demands for an apology. They were refused. Khrushchev, on the first day of the conference, made an angry attack on American policy and walked out. The Soviet delegates went home; the conference was in ruins, and East-West tensions were increased rather than reduced. Agreement on a German peace treaty was once more postponed.

Powers was later exchanged for the Soviet master-spy, Rudolf Abel.

New Weapons Vitally Affect the Cold War

The Growing Atomic Arsenal

With East and West in frantic competition, there was a race to gain new or improved weapons. In the 1950s 'nuclear' cannon were deployed. They could aim atomic shells at enemy forces. These were 'battlefield' or 'tactical' nuclear weapons. Though the possible use of these was bad enough, the search was also on for more effective 'strategic' nuclear weapons. These were large atomic bombs or warheads intended for use, as a last resort, against important targets in the enemy's homeland. Aircraft and rockets of greater size and range were developed by both East and West to carry them.

Some of the new developments had a powerful, direct effect on the world situation, and therefore on the Cold War. Although they were all in the end closely related, here are two brief 'case studies'.

The Case of the Inter-Continental Rocket

The USSR produced the first ICBM (Inter-Continental Ballistic Missile) in 1957 (see p. 101). From its launch site in the USSR it could, if needed, reach the United States. When stockpiles of these giant rockets had been built up, the USA would be directly threatened. This had never been so before, and it produced a change in American thinking. There was an immense pressure to close the 'missile gap'. Vast sums of money were poured into rocket development. There was pressure also to locate the Soviet rocket bases, so that they could be 'targeted' by the giant bombers of the American Strategic Air Command. U-2 flights over the USSR were authorised partly for this purpose. And the 'missile gap' was later proved to have been an illusion. The USSR was not, after all, very far ahead of the USA in large rocket development. Clearly, the arms race was gaining an impetus of its own. There was a danger that weapons, rather than the political leaders, might dictate events.

The Case of the Nuclear-Powered, Nuclear-Armed Submarine

In 1955 the Americans installed a nuclear reactor in a submarine. Its range was thereby extended beyond any submariner's wildest dreams. A piece of radioactive material no larger than a tennis ball provided power enough to circumnavigate the world. What is more, the vessel could stay submerged for very long periods, since the tennis ball did not need air to function. The crew could breathe using purified air, with oxygen supplied from storage flasks, or sucked in whilst the boat was close to the surface. A submarine cruising at high speeds below the surface, and for weeks on end, could go almost anywhere. What enemy could know where it had got to?

One further possibility beckoned the naval planners. Submarines could already be fitted with short-range 'cruise' missiles, fired from the surface. What if the nuclear-powered boats could become mobile, under-water launch platforms for large rockets — say with a range of 1600 kilometres or more?

One of the American boats was cut in half. A new section, 40 metres long, was added. It contained a battery of large vertical tubes, designed to take rockets. On 20 July 1960 the *USS George Washington* successfully fired a Polaris missile from below the surface. A new type of capital ship had been born.

The Soviets quickly followed the American lead. By the late 1960s Soviet submarines could lie off the east or west coasts of the USA, their atomic missiles capable of devastating much of the country. American submarines, some based in a Scottish loch, could lurk in the Arctic or the Eastern Mediterranean, their rockets 'locked on' targets in European Russia. On top of this, both Britain and France built their own smaller fleets of missile-carrying submarines.

All this had tremendous consequences. First, there was the enormous cost — billions of dollars or roubles which might

The USS *Sam Rayburn* is seen here with her sixteen missile silos open. Each housed a Polaris rocket, with atomic warhead, for underwater launching

have been more constructively used. Secondly, these were clearly 'strategic' rather than battlefield weapons. They threatened bases and cities far inland. This produced a new situation: neither East nor West could ever hope to win a nuclear war. Whatever might happen if such a war broke out, enough nuclear submarines on either side would survive to carry out a 'second strike'. Even the heaviest surprise attack would only ensure the attacker's own destruction.

The arrival of the Polaris-type submarine produced a decisive change in the attitudes of world leaders. Their main concern could only be the prevention of nuclear war; everything else had to come second. After about 1960 the speeches of Presidents Kennedy or Johnson, or Prime Ministers Khrushchev or Kosygin, clearly show this. A new weapon had changed the strategy and the thinking of the Cold War.

9 The Cold War World-wide and Space-wide

Containment in Asia

South East-Asia: The Domino Theory

The Cold War had started in Europe, when the armies had met, and the Allies had disagreed. It had been extended to Asia when Mao triumphed in China and the North Koreans invaded South Korea. But it was also being fought in South-East Asia, in Indo-China.

Indo-China had been part of the French Empire, and from 1946 the French were fighting to re-establish their control. Their opponents were the communist armies of Ho Chi Minh. Ho was a Vietnamese communist who had studied in Moscow. He had spent years organising and preparing for a revolution in Indo-China. From 1950 Truman's US government gave aid to the French in their struggle with Ho's forces; this policy was continued after 1953 by Eisenhower. Eisenhower likened the situation in South-East Asia to a row of dominoes: if one country fell, others would surely follow:

'You have a row of dominoes set up. You knock over the first one, and what will happen to the last one is the certainty that it will go over very quickly... Asia, after all, has already lost some 450 millions of its peoples to the communist dictatorship, and we simply can't afford greater losses.'

(7 April 1954)

The Geneva Agreements

The US concern about communism led to some fateful decisions. A conference held in Geneva in 1954 decided that in future Indo-China would be divided into the completely independent states of Laos, Cambodia and Vietnam. It was the end of the French Empire in South-East Asia. As a

111

temporary measure Vietnam was to be split into two, since all North Vietnam was already under firm communist control. Elections would be held to decide on a future government for the whole country. But the US refused to sign the final Geneva agreements, since the elections would plainly result in a communist triumph — for North Vietnam had the greater part of the population. The division of Vietnam persisted.

A Chain of Alliances: from NATO to SEATO

After the French defeat in Indo-China in 1954, the main western powers joined in forming SEATO: the South-East Asia Treaty Organisation. It included Pakistan, Thailand, the Philippines, New Zealand and Australia, as well as Britain, France and the USA. Its purpose was to resist further communist expansion, though there were also economic provisions which were intended to assist the trade of the poorer members. France and Pakistan both withdrew support from SEATO after 1965 — they did not wish to be involved in the Vietnam War. SEATO was ended in 1975.

Another regional alliance created at this time (1955) was the Baghdad Pact. This linked Turkey, Iraq, Iran and Pakistan. Britain was also a member, and the USA joined the military and economic side of the Pact. The members formed a 'girdle' from the Mediterranean to the mountain barrier of the Himalayas.

The Encirclement of the USSR

The West saw these arrangements as defensive. Soviet statesmen saw them very differently: as part of an attempt to encircle the USSR. NATO had been the first part of the chain of encirclement, they said, the US–Japanese Security Pact of 1951 had been the second; SEATO and the Baghdad Pact were the last links. Khrushchev again and again referred to these alliances, and the US bases which existed within many of the alliance states, as a pistol held at the head of the USSR. 'Can we,' he said, 'disregard actions by the governments of the Western Powers such as the establishment of a network of US military bases along the frontiers of the Soviet Union, and of countries friendly to it?'

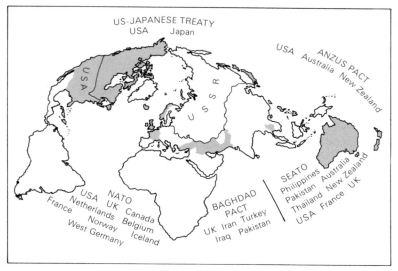

The ring of alliances which Khrushchev and other Soviet leaders claimed was a threat to the USSR and its allies. Membership of the alliances changed over the Cold War years, eg Iraq withdrew from the Baghdad Pact in 1959, when it was re-named the Central Treaty Organisation. SEATO was ended in 1975, but both France and Pakistan had ceased to be active members ten years earlier

The Vietnam War

Great Power Support for the Two Sides in Vietnam

The Geneva Agreements brought only a brief respite to Indo-China. The communists controlled North Vietnam, and they trained and supported guerilla movements in the South, contrary to the Agreements. These guerillas eventually became known as the Viet Cong. They terrorised villages and country districts into supporting them with food, shelter, information and recruits. China and the USSR gave aid to North Vietnam and the guerillas; the USA helped South Vietnam.

'The United States will Stand by its Friends'

American assistance to South Vietnam was greatly increased in 1961. Over three thousand officers were sent to advise and

113

train the South's army and other forces. Both President Kennedy, who was assassinated in 1963, and President Johnson were determined to resist any further advance of communism in Asia. This is how Johnson saw the situation:

'The battle against Communism must be joined in South-East Asia with the strength and determination to achieve success... we must decide whether to help these countries to the best of our ability or throw in the towel... and pull back our defences to San Francisco and a Fortress America concept.'

The USA, said Johnson, would stand by its friends. South Vietnam was an ally under the South-East Asia Treaty (see p. 112).

One difficulty about helping South Vietnam was the weakness of its governments. After 1963, coup followed coup; many Chief Ministers lasted no more than six weeks. When free elections were held, though they showed little support for communism they also showed the people to be hopelessly divided in their support for various political and religious groups. There were over twenty parties. Furthermore, any South Vietnam government was badly hampered by the Viet Cong's campaign of murder and kidnapping against all government employees.

The US Joins the Shooting War: an 'Open Ended Commitment'

In 1964 there were brief clashes between US and North Vietnamese naval vessels in the Gulf of Tonkin, and the US replied with air attacks on northern coastal bases. The US Congress gave President Johnson power to take any necessary steps 'to prevent further aggression'.

By early 1965 large areas were under communist control — in the north, central and southern parts of South Vietnam, including areas very close to the large cities. It was clear that South Vietnam was doomed unless the USA joined the war in earnest. Using the powers given him by Congress, Johnson ordered troops to Vietnam. Marines arrived to defend the air base at Da Nang in March 1965, and a rapid build-up followed. Johnson warned that the USA would give its aid 'to any in South-East Asia who ask our help in defending their freedom'. Johnson's opponents warned that this was a rash promise—an 'open ended commitment'.

American forces poured into South Vietnam—half a million by the end of 1967. Alongside them fought the South Vietnamese forces, about 700,000 men. Other states also sent troops: South Korea, Australia, New Zealand, the Philippines and Thailand—perhaps another 50,000 in all. Britain supported the US action, but refused to join 'the shooting war'.

Modern Technology in a Poor Country

The USA brought enormous resources into the Vietnam War. Supply bases, ports and airfields were constructed:

'In 1965 South Vietnam had one major port... By 1968 there were seven deep-water ports...and many smaller ports. Where once there were three jet runways...by 1968 there were fifteen... In addition, there were more than 200 smaller airfields and almost 200 heliports. Major construction of storage depots, hospitals, communications sites, roads and bridges was being completed in record time.'

The US also used an enormous range of weapons: giant B-52 bombers; tanker planes which sprayed the jungle to destroy the leaf cover on which the Viet Cong relied. Electronic sensors were planted across battlefields to report automatically any movement, and gunsights were invented which could see through the darkest night. At the war's height about 3500 helicopters were in use for transport and aerial attack.

North Vietnam also used more and more powerful weapons. They included very heavy artillery and rockets, Soviet PT76 tanks, and Mig fighter planes, as well as flame-throwers. But despite this vast effort, it was 'low technology' which was vital. Most of the supplies were carried into the South by man-power, or ferried on thousands of cargo bicycles along the Ho Chi Minh trail.

115

Indo-China: communist armies or guerillas struggled to dominate the new states of Laos, Cambodia and Vietnam

The Pacification Programme

The US tried hard to win the 'economic and social war', as well as the shooting war. It supplied vast amounts of aid to try to 'settle' the countryside, making the peasants prosperous and loyal. Teams of South Vietnamese were trained and sent to selected areas. In addition to stiffening resistance to the Viet Cong, they supervised the building of schools and health centres, and the supply of cattle, pigs and chickens to help farmers start afresh. Tools and seed were given, and wells dug.

The pacification programme was partially successful, but it was hastily devised and had too little time in which to work. In some country districts the Viet Cong's hold was weakened or eliminated; but it could return at any time.

A War Without Fixed Battle Lines

The North's army became more and more directly involved in the fighting in South Vietnam. Together with the Viet Cong they would make sharp raids or assaults on villages, cities and bases held by the South and the Americans. In the worst and most prolonged assaults great damage was done, US stores or aircraft destroyed, and casualties were heavy. Some developed into full-scale battles, lasting weeks on end.

The South's forces and the Americans made their own sweeps into the communist-held areas. They used 'search and destroy' patrols, often relying on helicopter transport. When Viet Cong were found, devastating air attacks could be called up if needed. There were thus no fixed battle lines in Vietnam — unlike many earlier wars.

The Tet Offensive, 1968

Communist forces launched their major offensive of the war during the 'Tet' holiday, celebrating the lunar new year, on 30 January 1968. More than thirty cities were attacked, as well as many US bases and loyal villages. In Saigon itself the Viet Cong entered the city from the nearby jungle and swamp areas. One group attacked the US embassy, another the President's palace, and still others an airfield. In other cities major buildings were captured for a time, and the communist radio claimed that the South's government was about to be destroyed.

All the attacks were thrown back, though the communists held on for weeks in some places. In Hué, in the north, they executed more than 1000 people holding government jobs, including teachers and minor civil servants, before their hold was broken.

Opposition to the Vietnam War in the USA

Public opinion polls showed that most Americans supported the American action in Vietnam in 1965. But by 1968 opposition had mounted. Enormous demonstrations against the war took place; the increasing casualties strengthened the doubters and protesters. The US kept its forces up to strength by conscription, and hundreds or thousands of young men showed their objections to the war by burning the draft cards which called them up. Congress revoked the wide powers to make war which it had earlier given the President, in June 1970. Respected politicians, church leaders and entertainers all called for American withdrawal from Vietnam.

Vietnamisation, and Peace Talks in Paris

The US government, bowing to the change in opinion inside the USA, decided that it must withdraw its troops gradually from the war. The South Vietnamese must take over their own defence. They called this policy 'Vietnamisation'. At the same time ceasefire talks began in Paris. The first of these, in 1968, was only made possible because the US greatly limited its air attacks on targets in North Vietnam. The first troops were withdrawn in June 1969, and in 1970 the US pulled completely out of the ground fighting. It continued its air support to the South.

Ceasefire: the USA Leaves the War

In 1973 the Paris talks produced an uneasy ceasefire. The last US troops left Vietnam, leaving only officials or advisers concerned with trade and aid. The South were left to defend themselves in any future fighting. US bases and stores were turned over to them.

By the time of the ceasefire, over fifty thousand Americans had been killed in Vietnam. Vietnamese casualties, both North and South, are unknown, but at least run into some hundreds of thousands.

A Soviet comment on the Vietnam war, 1965. The escalators are marked 'From Vietnam' and 'To Vietnam'

The Communist Triumph in Indo-China

The ceasefire was broken frequently by both sides. The North continued to occupy large parts of the country, and early in 1975 they commenced a widespread offensive. The South's forces made some initial resistance, but then disintegrated and fled. The remaining Americans were evacuated by sea or air, together with some of the Vietnamese who had worked closely with them. On 30 April the communist forces entered Saigon and set up a 'Provisional Revolutionary Government'. The following year the whole country, both North and South, was declared to be the 'Socialist Republic of Vietnam'.

1975 also saw the triumph of communist armies in Laos and Cambodia, encouraged and helped by the North Vietnamese. The domino effect of which Eisenhower had spoken had thus come into play. The American intervention in Vietnam had delayed, but not stopped, the victory of communism in South-East Asia.

119

The Communist Challenge in the Developing World

By the mid-1950s it was clear that the Cold War was in many ways a struggle for people's minds. This was nowhere more true than in countries which had just gained their independence, or were about to gain it. As the old British, French, Dutch and, later, Portuguese empires broke up, new states with new leaders and new names appeared. Both Soviet and Chinese leaders hoped to win these for communism. The newly independent states sometimes faced a difficult choice. They badly needed aid to develop their industry, or agriculture, or education, or commerce. To obtain such help, should they link themselves with the USSR, with China, or with one of the Western powers?

'Neo-colonialism'

Stalin refused to believe that the colonies of Britain and France would ever be genuinely freed. Communists regarded India (independent in 1947) or even Ghana (independent in 1957) as still tied economically to their former masters. Though no longer full colonies, they were 'neocolonies' — dominated in a new way from Britain. But about 1960 new African states were gaining independence by the dozen, and communists were forced to change their views. The Chinese and Soviets set out to befriend these countries and to influence them politically.

The 'Scramble' for Influence in the Developing World

The Russians gave aid, or arms, to India, Egypt, Indonesia, Ethiopia, Algeria and Syria. They made a point of sending large delegations to attend the independence ceremonies as the former colonies were freed. They went to great lengths to train diplomats in native African languages. Mali, Guinea and Ghana received generous assistance with their commerce. By 1975 a Soviet magazine commented that

'thousands of Soviet people are selflessly working in Africa. Doctors, geologists, teachers and people of many other occupations are to be met with in Algeria, Sierra Leone, Ethiopia, Guinea, Nigeria, the Congo and Tanzania, and other countries. They are willingly sharing their vast know-how with nations that were denied friendly help for many decades... The Soviet Union and other Socialist countries are Africa's dependable allies in the struggle against the forces of imperialism, neo-colonialism and racism.'

Along with Soviet aid there went requests for the use of airfields or ports. The USSR gained the use of bases in Egypt in this way, and in 1960–2 made similar arrangements with Guinea, in west Africa, and Somalia, in east Africa. They also helped the Cubans to place troops and advisers in a dozen African countries.

China, too, made great efforts in Africa. The Chinese believed that their own communist revolution provided the best example for the new states to follow. Chinese experts visited many countries, especially Ethiopia, Zambia, Tanzania, the Congo and Ghana. In Zambia and Tanzania they provided the cash and engineers for a gigantic project: a railway from the port of Dar-es-Salaam to mining areas of Zambia. It is 1760 km long, and has 2500 bridges and viaducts — a magnificent achievement in difficult country.

The Tan-Zam Railway crosses from Tanzania to Zambia. The track-laying machine, supervised by Chinese engineers, has laid the last metals on the Tanzanian side, and is about to lay the first on the Zambian side. August 1973

Both the USSR and China supplied arms to the developing countries, and trained some of their soldiers. By 1965 Soviet or eastern-bloc weapons equipped many African armies, including those of Egypt, Algeria, Somalia and Tanzania. And

'there were...by 1966, about 2500 tanks in North Africa and the Middle East, or approximately the same number as that used by Nazi Germany to conquer France and the Low Countries in 1940.'

Students from the developing world began to go to the USSR in ever greater numbers from about 1955 onwards. They were given free board, money for personal expenses, and were trained — without charge — in engineering, agriculture, medicine, chemistry and similar fields.

Soviet-Chinese rivalry in Africa was obvious to everybody. President Nyerere of Tanzania called it 'a second scramble for Africa' in 1964.

The Two Vessels

Communist attitudes to the developing world are well explained by a remark of Khrushchev:

'The world consists of socialist and capitalist countries. They can be regarded as two communicating vessels. At present, as regards the number of states, the capitalist vessel is fuller. But this is a temporary state of affairs. History is developing in a way which will reduce the level in the capitalist vessel, while the socialist vessel will get fuller.'

Spies of the Cold War: 6 Spy Satellites

From about 1960 onwards the two superpowers gained the ability to watch one another's territory using satellites. Development of these was extremely rapid, Sputnik 1 having been launched only three years earlier.

SAMOS and Cosmos: Watchers from the Sky

One day in 1964 a Thor rocket blasts off from its launch-pad at the US Air Force Vandenberg base in California. It is one

'The Sweep Out!' A Soviet cartoonist's view of decolonialisation in Africa

of a series, launched at more or less regular intervals over a period of years. In a minute or so its roar can no longer be heard; then, after a few moments more, it has disappeared from sight. From that point onwards it is tracked by radar.

At a height of perhaps 240 km a SAMOS* satellite is detached from the rocket and thrust into earth orbit. It will fly round the earth along a precise path, shaped like a huge ellipse. At its lowest point, possibly eighty miles above earth's surface, it will also be over its main target area within the Soviet Union. The orbit has been carefully calculated, and corrected, so that the SAMOS arrives just when the sun

* SAMOS = Satellite and Missile Observation Systems

is in the best position to obtain excellent, side-lit photographs. What is more, on future days and during corresponding 'passes', it will repeat its photographs when the sun's rays are again at this exact angle.

SAMOS carries a camera of outstanding performance. The pictures taken will reveal every building in a camp, and every vehicle. When conditions are good, individual humans can be seen and counted. The length of the cast shadows will betray the height of buildings, and the rate of progress with any new construction. By the time the SAMOS mission is completed and the photographs interpreted, it has revealed the story of Soviet activity over a period of perhaps fourteen or twenty days in the target area.

SAMOS satellites have their Soviet counterparts, doing similar work over the USA for the Soviet Union. They have the name Cosmos (= world), and among other targets they watch the US missile launch bases, naval and military camps, and the movement of ships and troops in NATO and other exercises.

'Open Skies' for Satellites

Since the 1960s the 'watch from the skies' has become more and more effective. Satellites can be 'stationed' exactly above their targets, relaying information to ground stations. They may be armed with infra-red cameras, and with sensors which can detect the heat produced by rockets. They can pick up and relay both radar and radio signals from far below. They can discover solid objects hidden under trees, or see whether fuel storage tanks are full or empty. Their cameras can produce pictures of almost unbelievable detail — enough, it is said, to tell whether human beings are in uniform.

Both superpowers have accepted the satellite age. The USSR does not destroy American satellites, nor do the Americans destroy Soviet satellites. This may even have eased the Cold War a little, since no side can now shield its military preparations from the other. This has been called the 'Open Skies' policy, after Eisenhower's abortive suggestion of 1955.

10 Easing the Cold War

The Search for Disarmament

Both East and West say they want disarmament and peace. Their efforts to limit arms have had a little success; but both have maintained and increased their enormous stocks of weapons, both ordinary and atomic.

The main efforts to control the arms race are as follows.

The Baruch Plan

This American plan for the complete control of atomic energy was put to the UN in 1946. It proposed an agency under UN control to cover all mining of uranium, all manufacture of weapons, and all uses of the atom for peaceful purposes. The USA offered to hand over to this agency its stocks of atomic bombs, and all details about manufacture. Stalin, and the USSR, rejected this plan. Stalin wanted stocks of bombs destroyed *first*, then the agency, with controls and inspections, set up. The plan failed because of this opposition, though the International Atomic Energy Agency was eventually created to deal with the peaceful uses of the atom (1956).

The Soviet and Western Plans of 1948–1949

The USSR suggested a one-third reduction in all armed forces, and abolition of all atomic weapons, in 1948. The USA and the West were unwilling to include atomic weapons in the scheme, since they felt threatened at the time by Soviet pressures in Europe. The Western plan, the following year, called for a census of all armed forces, and a UN control body to watch them. The USSR rejected this since it did not cover atomic weapons.

The Western Plan of 1954

The British and French suggested a step-by-step reduction in all types of arms, with a rigid inspection system to check progress.

The Soviet Offer of 1955

The USSR partly accepted the British-French plan, and added its own scheme. Arms and armies would be reduced during the first year; nuclear tests would halt. In the second year there would be more reductions and the destruction of all atomic weapons. This Soviet plan allowed for international inspection.

The Open Skies Plan of 1955

President Eisenhower offered during a Geneva conference to open the USA to Soviet inspection, giving all facilities for aerial photography from American airports. This was provided the USSR would do the same.

1955 was the 'high-spot' of disarmament efforts. The Soviet and American plans looked as if they might lead to genuine arms reductions, perhaps in some combined form. But the USA then had doubts, feeling that to put inspectors in ports and on railway stations, as the USSR suggested, was not good enough. They wanted the full 'open skies' system, from which the USSR shied away. The schemes were allowed to drop. The UN's disarmament sub-committee, which had considered these last schemes, broke up in disagreement in 1957.

The 'Atom Treaties' of the 1960s

Further efforts dealt with small parts of the arms problem, rather than the whole problem itself.

The first arms agreement of any kind since the Second World War came in 1958, when the two super-powers and some others agreed that Antarctica should be nuclear-free. A second hopeful sign was the Test-Ban Treaty of 1963. By this the USA, USSR and Britain halted all nuclear tests, except underground ones. France and China refused to join this treaty—they were about to conduct tests of their own. The first French bomb was exploded in 1960; the Chinese in 1964.

In 1968 came a further step forward with a 'Nuclear Non-Proliferation' Treaty, by which states agreed not to seek nuclear weapons, nor to help others to obtain them. The major powers signed; some states, like India and South Africa, did not. India exploded a nuclear bomb in 1974.

The SALT Agreements

The problem of the atomic and other weapons possessed by the super-powers remained. In the 1970s the first small steps were taken towards restricting them. The two powers limited themselves in defence systems against rockets in 1972. The cost of such anti-rocket defences was too enormous for them to contemplate. Also in 1972 came the SALT I agreement (SALT = Strategic Arms Limitation Talks). This 'froze' for five years the numbers of large rockets, both on land and in submarines, possessed by the USA and USSR. Bombers were not covered. Talks held from 1977 onwards for a new 'SALT' agreement resulted in a treaty in 1979 limiting every type of rocket, and the numbers of warheads. This meant that each side would have to dismantle a few existing large rockets, in order to keep within SALT II's limits. Though both sides kept to these terms, the USA refused to ratify the treaty: it remained only an unofficial guide.

Détente

Lessening World Tensions

Khrushchev fell from power in 1964, on the same day that China exploded her first atomic bomb. Khrushchev's successors continued the peaceful coexistence policy, saying they would compete with the West without war.

East-West relations were soured by two world crises in the late 1960s: a third Arab-Israeli war in 1967, and the Soviet invasion of Czechoslovakia in 1968. But by 1969 both sides were talking of the need for 'détente'.

Détente means a lessening of tensions. There was good reason to seek this. After Cuba, after the crises of 1967–1968, both sides realised the danger of a plunge into war through mishap or misunderstanding. There were other reasons for détente as well:

1 The colossal cost of the arms race. By 1969 the two superpowers were about equal in nuclear weapons. The Soviet leader, Brezhnev, could feel he was dealing with the USA as an equal.

2 There had been a small-scale détente between East and West Germany, and West Germany agreed in 1969 not to seek nuclear weapons. This laid to rest one of the greatest Soviet fears — a nuclear-armed West Germany.

3 The Americans were cutting down their troops in Vietnam from 1969 onwards. The new American President, Richard Nixon, called for better relations with the USSR.

4 The USSR had a serious 'China problem' on its hands. The two Red Armies had fought battles in border lands which the Tsars had wrested from China a century earlier. There seemed a possibility of full-scale war. In view of this, the USSR urgently needed to ease relations with the USA.

Both sides entered the 1970s saying they would do everything possible for détente — allowing the world to breathe a little more freely.

The Struggle Will Continue . . . Without Wars

Détente was only an idea — but it was a step towards a safer world. However, it did not remove the basic differences between East and West. Leonid Brezhnev's view of détente in 1973 was that the class struggle of the two systems would continue, in economics, in politics, and in the realm of ideas. 'But,' he said, 'we shall strive to shift this historically inevitable struggle onto a path free from the perils of War.'

A more cynical, western view of détente was put by a later British Foreign Minister. He had seen Soviet troops invade Afghanistan. He said 'The Soviet conception of détente is that short of war you can do anything you like' (Lord Carrington, 1981).

The Loosening of the Alliances

'Poly-Centric' Communism

From 1945 to 1948 there had been but one communist world. It was dominated by the USSR, and directed by Stalin.

In 1948 the quarrel with Yugoslavia broke into the open, and at Stalin's insistence Yugoslavia was expelled from the Cominform and from the Eastern bloc. Tito then showed that a communist state could exist quite outside Moscow's control — if it were in the right geographical position, beyond easy reach of Soviet armies.

After 1949, with Mao's China seemingly in complete agreement with Stalin, the communist bloc looked worldwide and menacing. It appeared to act with a single purpose, and to present a powerful threat to the rest of the world.

By 1960 the USSR and China had disagreed; by 1969 there was even a chance of war between them. Their leaders argued about the correct interpretation of Marxism-Leninism. But their actions looked more and more like those of Great Powers striving for mastery or pre-eminence.

The communists of the world were yet more split than this. The Romanians had managed to gain some independence of the USSR by 1970. They wished to develop their trade in Romania's own interests, and did not fall in with Soviet plans for the 'integration' of the commerce and industry of all the communist bloc states. Neither did they follow the USSR in its condemnation of Mao's China in the 1960s. The Polish communists had also begun to develop their own views a few years after Stalin's death. They laid great stress on 'the Polish path to Socialism', which clearly meant that they had no intention of sticking closely to the Soviet path, if they could avoid it. In addition to these signs that the USSR's control was not absolutely complete, there occurred the Hungarian revolt in 1956 and the Prague Spring in 1968 (see pp. 79 and 91). It was plain that there was disagreement and even rebellion among the members of the Warsaw Pact, though none of them could hope to escape the enormous influence of the USSR. Outside the east European bloc the communist parties in Italy and France had also shown independence, openly disagreeing with Moscow on the ways in which the revolution they expected would come to their countries. They refused simply to accept Soviet views or Soviet orders. Communism had developed many varieties. It was no longer centred purely on Moscow. People said it had become 'poly-centric' — many-centred.

NATO's Problems

NATO too had suffered changes which weakened it. France had withdrawn her forces from the NATO command, and asked for the removal of NATO military bases, in 1966–7. Britain's strength had declined greatly since the immediate post-war years. The development of inter-continental rockets meant that the USA had to respond to the threat of a

Die Ko-Existenz

A West German view of the two alliances in the 1950s. The Warsaw Pact ('Ost-NATO') is under strict discipline, whilst the democratic West is in disarray

possible direct attack on her home territory, rather than just to a possible Soviet thrust into western Europe. And the chain of alliances which had extended 'containment' to the Far East had been badly affected — Pakistan had become more friendly towards China, and Iraq had left the Baghdad Pact in 1959 after a revolution.

The NATO commanders had another worry. About 1960 there grew up in the West groups of people who protested against nuclear arms, and wished their countries to give them up irrespective of Warsaw Pact policies. Some of these unilateral nuclear disarmers also wished their countries to leave NATO altogether. Inevitably, they were joined by pro-communist groups whose real motives were to weaken the West's position. The anti-nuclear movements failed to change any NATO policies, and their influence waned after the Cuba Crisis; but they continued as a sizeable minority which might affect future policy.

Despite the 'cracks' in the two power-blocs, there remained no doubt about one thing. Each would still act, if faced by some crisis in which the other seemed to threaten it directly. The alliances might be looser, and tensions might have lessened, but if 'crisis-management' were ever to fail, they could still virtually destroy one another.

11 Interpretations

Ways of Looking at the Cold War

There are many ways of looking at the Cold War, and we should be aware of the main ones. These are summarized below.

The 'Truman' View

According to this, it was the USSR which deliberately broke up the effort to create a unified, peaceful world after 1945. Stalin's takeover of the east European countries was merely his first step. His determined plan was to extend communism everywhere, by fair means or foul — usually foul. In extending communism, he would also be extending the USSR's 'sphere of influence' — only the sphere would be world-wide. Stalin did not care about honesty in politics — as a communist he believed that 'the end justifies the means.' Neither did he care for the ideals of the United Nations, whose proper working was repeatedly blocked by Soviet action. And he was quite prepared to break up the wartime comradeship with the USA and Britain, once he could get no more out of it.

The free world had to stop this threat. It began to oppose it firmly with the Berlin airlift, the creation of NATO, and with its action in Korea.

Winston Churchill took this view. President Truman acted on it. Stalin and the other Soviet leaders took all the blame.

The 'USSR in Search of Security' View

This view regards most of the Soviet actions after 1945 as highly understandable. The USSR had repeatedly suffered from terrible invasions. Most had come via eastern Europe. The German invasion of 1941–4 was by far the worst. The devastation and the casualties were on an immense, horrifying scale. It was only to be expected that the Soviets would ensure against further horrors by making quite certain that east European governments were friendly. This is the true reason for the Soviet domination there — the communist side of it is incidental. The West ought to take these things into account, realising that the Soviet search for security after 1945 was not a plot to take over the world.

The beginnings of this attitude go back to the US Department of the Treasury in the days when Henry Morgenthau was Roosevelt's Secretary there (1939–45). Morgenthau continued to serve President Truman, till July 1945. He was well aware of the effects Soviet suffering would have on their post-war policies. Though Morgenthau's influence was removed in July 1945, there were to be other American and British statesmen who took the same view, particularly after 1950.

The View of the 'Revisionists'

Some Western thinkers have completely revised both the former ways of seeing the Cold War. They point out that the USA, in 1945, had become by far the most powerful nation in the world. As far as most industrial goods were concerned, she could out-produce the rest of the world put together. Remember, both Germany and Japan were no longer rivals. America was in fact a commercial giant. Even this does not fully describe US power — one author called her 'The Free World Colossus'.* Her influence would plainly be immense. She would not, as in pre-war days, be isolationist, but concerned with the rest of the world as never before. And she possessed the atom bomb.

America, in this new world role of commercial giant, was concerned to build up business interests everywhere. The influence of her thousands upon thousands of firms dominated American policies, whether statesmen admitted it or

---

* D.Horowitz, *The Free World Colossus*, MacGibbon and Kee, 1965

not. Her businessmen were constructing a universal 'commercial empire.' Her vast wealth, and sometimes the CIA, were used to influence foreign governments in ways favourable to the USA. American lip-service to the United Nations and freedom were mere self-deception or hypocrisy.

The Cold War arose from Stalin's response to this situation. His seizure of eastern Europe was a search for security and an answer to the threat of the atom bomb.

This view shifts the blame for the Cold War onto the USA. The culprit was American aggressive capitalism. Those who took this view were influenced by the war which the USA fought in Vietnam in the 1960s and early 1970s. Far from American shores, it seemed to confirm their theories.

Although the first of these views—the 'Truman' interpretation—is the one most usually accepted in the West we should bear in mind all three, in thinking about events after 1945. Some parts of the Cold War may seem to fit the first view best; others the second or third. There may be strands of truth in all three.

Communism: a 'Conflict View' of the World

Communist theory, at least up to Stalin's death in 1953, was simple: wars are caused only by capitalist countries. Socialist states cannot cause wars, since their policies are based on international brotherhood and cooperation. This view was so obviously inadequate to explain the tensions and conflicts which occurred around the world in the 1950s and 1960s that it has been under continual discussion and argument among communists.

An official, Soviet version of the post-war development of the Cold War is that the USSR wanted 'peaceful cooperation between countries', but this

'did not enter into the calculations of the aggressive imperialist circles who charted US foreign policy after the war. The US rulers rejected the Soviet peace proposals and took the line of suppressing the liberation struggle of the working class and oppressed peoples throughout the world, and forming military and political blocs against the USSR and

134

the People's Democracies, drawing the capitalist countries dependent on the USA into the orbit of their adventurist policies.'

This is perhaps best described as a conflict view of the world. According to it, the West is completely to blame; the USSR is blameless. This view is the only one found in Soviet books. The expression 'The Cold War' is used to mean Western criticisms of the USSR, or Western policies the USSR does not like. The Soviet view is therefore that their country is the victim of the Cold War — it does not contribute to it in any way. When Soviets appeal for an end to the Cold War, they are asking only for a change in Western policies or attitudes, and are not implying that the USSR will change its own policies.

Are the Roots of the Cold War Older than the Twentieth Century?

'Great Russian Imperialism'

Over the centuries Tsarist Russia had expanded enormously. Originally a restricted area around Moscow, it came by 1914 to be the world's largest state, though a backward one. After the 1917 revolution, though interrupted for a time, this tendency to expand simply continued. But now it was directed by a ruthless and determined communist government. Thus the Soviet pressure on surrounding states may be seen merely as a resumption of the policies of the eighteenth and nineteeth centuries.

The USSR and the West: Different Civilizations

The habits of thought of Russians and Westerners are dissimilar, it is said, in vital ways. Though rulers like Ivan the Terrible (1533–84) and Peter the Great (1682–1725) were eager to borrow Western crafts and Western ideas, basically they thought of Russia as self-sufficient and superior. Russia might 'Westernise', but it would always be completely distinct. On top of this, there is 'the centuries-old Russian suspicion of foreigners, so deep as to be almost second nature'. According to this view, expressed here by A.J.P. Taylor, East and West were opposed, competing civilisations:

'The Cold War is older than the Second World War, older even than the Bolshevik revolution. It goes back at least to the great schism, which long ago divided the Orthodox and Roman Catholic churches, and brought such misfortunes in the Middle Ages. During the nineteenth century rivalry, suspicion and war were the normal relations between Great Britain and Russia. In the twentieth century fear of Germany twice drove Russia and the Western Powers into an uneasy alliance. Once that fear was removed the two civilisations reverted to their normal relations which we now like to call the Cold War.'

Of course, the West too assumed that it was superior. This was particularly true from the time of the Industrial Revolution onwards, which was a Western feature. The growth of parliaments and democratic government in the West was another field in which the USSR and the East seemed unlikely ever to match Britain, France or the United States. The West was prosperous and democratic; the USSR was backward and used to the absolute rule of the Tsars. These differences persisted after the communists came to power. The two systems could hardly exist side by side without comparisons being made, so that ultimately changes in one or both would result.

Spheres of Influence

The Cold War is often connected with the nineteenth-century idea of 'spheres of influence'. Just as, a hundred years ago, Great Powers struggled to establish areas where their interests would prevail, so it is possible to see the two superpowers as being engaged in an updated version of this struggle. The difference between the nineteenth-century situation and the Cold War is that the competitors are now limited to two — or three if we include China — and that modern communications and weapons have both extended the spheres and increased the dangers of the policy.

Index

Index

Khrushchev N., 65–70, 72, 77, 84, 87, 91, 98, 107, 110, 112, 122, 127
Korea, 58–61, 65, 74, 111, 115, 132
Kosygin A., 110

Lend-Lease, 13–14
Lenin V. I., 16, 62, 69
London Conference (1947), 24–5
Lonsdale G., 94–7, 99
Lublin, 7

MacArthur D., 60
Macmillan H., 107
Mao Tse-tung, 54–6, 72, 111, 129
Marshall G., Plan, 15–17, 21, 25–6, 32, 40, 42–4, 64
Marx K., Marxism, 16, 20, 62
Masaryk J., 32–3
McCarthyism, 63
Mindszenty J., 79, 82–3
Molotov V., 24–5, 35, 43–4, 61
Morganthau H., 133
Moscow Conference (1947), 24

Nagy I., 29, 80, 82–3
Nasser G. A., 84–5
NATO, 51–5, 64, 73, 84–5, 104–6, 112, 124, 130–2
Neo-colonialism, 120
New Course (Hungary), 80
New Zealand, 112, 115
Nigeria, 120
Nixon R., 128
NSC 68, 57–8
Nyerere J., 122

Oder-Neisse Line, 12–13
Open Skies policy, 124, 126

Pakistan, 107, 112, 131
Paris summit (1960), 107; Vietnam talks, 118
Pearson L., 52–3
Penkovsky O., 97–9
Philippines, 57, 112, 115
Pigs, Bay of, 85–6, 100
Poland, 7–9, 12, 18, 27–31, 34–5, 42, 45, 64, 68, 91, 100, 129
Polaris rocket, 109–10
Pomerania, 9, 12, 45, 73
Potsdam, 4, 8, 9
Powers F., 106–8
Prague, 23, 32–3, 91, 129

Rakosi M., 29, 31
Reparations, 8–9, 13, 34, 45
Romania, 12, 27–9, 64, 92, 129
Roosevelt F. D., 5–8, 45, 64, 133

SALT Agreements (1972 and 1979), 127
SEATO, 112
Senate, US, 63–4
Silesia, 9, 12, 45, 73
Socialist realism, 21
South Africa, 127
Soviet-German Pact (1939), 18
Sputnik, 94, 101–4, 122
Stalin J. V., 6–9, 12, 14, 17–22, 24, 30–2, 34, 38–9, 56, 65–8, 79, 120, 125, 129, 132, 134
Strategic Air Command (US), 88, 108
Suez, 72, 84

Taiwan, 56, 65
Tanzania, 120–2
Test Ban Treaty (1963), 69, 126
Tet offensive, 117
Thailand, 112, 115
Tito, 21, 28, 37–8, 68, 92, 129
Truman H., 8–9, 14, 22, 35, 39–41, 52, 56–60, 62, 64, 111, 132–3
Turkey, 5, 39–40, 53–4, 60, 112
Tydings committee (US), 63

U2 aircraft, 86–7, 100, 106–8
Unilateralism, 131
United Nations, 7, 23, 53; and Cuba, 88–90; Disarmament, 125–6; Hungary, 83; Korea, 58–60; Suez, 84; USA, 134; Veto, 25–6, 35, 56, 59, 132

Vandenberg A., 40
Viet Cong, 113–17
Vietnam, 111–19, 128, 134
Voice of America broadcasts, 72

Warsaw Pact, 38, 64, 82, 91, 129, 131
Washington missile conference (1957), 101–2

X Article, 19

Yalta Conference (1945), 4–8, 45
Yugoslavia, 21, 27–8, 37, 64, 129

Zambia, 121
Zhdanov A, 20–2